HowExpert Presents

Female World Tr ▮▮▮)1

How to ▮ n New Cultures, ▮▮▮ ▮▮▮ the World as a Solo Woman Traveler From A to Z!

HowExpert with Rebecca Friedberg

**Copyright HowExpert™
www.HowExpert.com**

For more tips related to this topic, visit HowExpert.com/femaletraveler.

Recommended Resources

- HowExpert.com – Quick 'How To' Guides on All Topics from A to Z by Everyday Experts.
- HowExpert.com/free – Free HowExpert Email Newsletter.
- HowExpert.com/books – HowExpert Books
- HowExpert.com/courses – HowExpert Courses
- HowExpert.com/membership – HowExpert Membership Site
- HowExpert.com/writers – Write About Your #1 Passion/Knowledge/Expertise & Become a HowExpert Author.
- HowExpert.com/resources – Additional HowExpert Recommended Resources
- YouTube.com/HowExpert – Subscribe to HowExpert YouTube.
- Instagram.com/HowExpert – Follow HowExpert on Instagram.
- Facebook.com/HowExpert – Follow HowExpert on Facebook.

COPYRIGHT, LEGAL NOTICE AND DISCLAIMER:

COPYRIGHT © BY HOWEXPERT™ (OWNED BY HOT METHODS). ALL RIGHTS RESERVED WORLDWIDE. NO PART OF THIS PUBLICATION MAY BE REPRODUCED IN ANY FORM OR BY ANY MEANS, INCLUDING SCANNING, PHOTOCOPYING, OR OTHERWISE WITHOUT PRIOR WRITTEN PERMISSION OF THE COPYRIGHT HOLDER.

DISCLAIMER AND TERMS OF USE: PLEASE NOTE THAT MUCH OF THIS PUBLICATION IS BASED ON PERSONAL EXPERIENCE AND ANECDOTAL EVIDENCE. ALTHOUGH THE AUTHOR AND PUBLISHER HAVE MADE EVERY REASONABLE ATTEMPT TO ACHIEVE COMPLETE ACCURACY OF THE CONTENT IN THIS GUIDE, THEY ASSUME NO RESPONSIBILITY FOR ERRORS OR OMISSIONS. ALSO, YOU SHOULD USE THIS INFORMATION AS YOU SEE FIT, AND AT YOUR OWN RISK. YOUR PARTICULAR SITUATION MAY NOT BE EXACTLY SUITED TO THE EXAMPLES ILLUSTRATED HERE; IN FACT, IT'S LIKELY THAT THEY WON'T BE THE SAME, AND YOU SHOULD ADJUST YOUR USE OF THE INFORMATION AND RECOMMENDATIONS ACCORDINGLY.

THE AUTHOR AND PUBLISHER DO NOT WARRANT THE PERFORMANCE, EFFECTIVENESS OR APPLICABILITY OF ANY SITES LISTED OR LINKED TO IN THIS BOOK. ALL LINKS ARE FOR INFORMATION PURPOSES ONLY AND ARE NOT WARRANTED FOR CONTENT, ACCURACY OR ANY OTHER IMPLIED OR EXPLICIT PURPOSE.

ANY TRADEMARKS, SERVICE MARKS, PRODUCT NAMES OR NAMED FEATURES ARE ASSUMED TO BE THE PROPERTY OF THEIR RESPECTIVE OWNERS, AND ARE USED ONLY FOR REFERENCE. THERE IS NO IMPLIED ENDORSEMENT IF WE USE ONE OF THESE TERMS.

NO PART OF THIS BOOK MAY BE REPRODUCED, STORED IN A RETRIEVAL SYSTEM, OR TRANSMITTED BY ANY OTHER MEANS: ELECTRONIC, MECHANICAL, PHOTOCOPYING, RECORDING, OR OTHERWISE, WITHOUT THE PRIOR WRITTEN PERMISSION OF THE AUTHOR.

ANY VIOLATION BY STEALING THIS BOOK OR DOWNLOADING OR SHARING IT ILLEGALLY WILL BE PROSECUTED BY LAWYERS TO THE FULLEST EXTENT. THIS PUBLICATION IS PROTECTED UNDER THE US COPYRIGHT ACT OF 1976 AND ALL OTHER APPLICABLE INTERNATIONAL, FEDERAL, STATE AND LOCAL LAWS AND ALL RIGHTS ARE RESERVED, INCLUDING RESALE RIGHTS: YOU ARE NOT ALLOWED TO GIVE OR SELL THIS GUIDE TO ANYONE ELSE.

THIS PUBLICATION IS DESIGNED TO PROVIDE ACCURATE AND AUTHORITATIVE INFORMATION WITH REGARD TO THE SUBJECT MATTER COVERED. IT IS SOLD WITH THE UNDERSTANDING THAT THE AUTHORS AND PUBLISHERS ARE NOT ENGAGED IN RENDERING LEGAL, FINANCIAL, OR OTHER PROFESSIONAL ADVICE. LAWS AND PRACTICES OFTEN VARY FROM STATE TO STATE AND IF LEGAL OR OTHER EXPERT ASSISTANCE IS REQUIRED, THE SERVICES OF A PROFESSIONAL SHOULD BE SOUGHT. THE AUTHORS AND PUBLISHER SPECIFICALLY DISCLAIM ANY LIABILITY THAT IS INCURRED FROM THE USE OR APPLICATION OF THE CONTENTS OF THIS BOOK.

COPYRIGHT BY HOWEXPERT™ (OWNED BY HOT METHODS)
ALL RIGHTS RESERVED WORLDWIDE.

Table of Contents

Recommended Resources..2
Introduction...6
Chapter 1: Trip Preparation...9
Mapping Your Travels..9
Vaccinations...11
Visas...12
Budget..13
Cell Phones..17
Travel Apps..20
Booking Your Flight...23
Choosing a Hostel..26
Health Insurance...29
Traveler's Insurance..31
Credit and Debit Cards..33
Staying in Touch with Friends and Family..............................37
Boyfriends and Girlfriends..38
Luggage..39
Packing...40
Birth Control..42
Chapter 2: How to Stay Safe..44
General Safety Tips..45
Couchsurfing..47
Hitchhiking...50
Travel Companions...51
"Safer" Countries..55
Europe..56
Middle East..59
Asia...62
North America...67
Central America..69
South America...71
Africa..73
Oceania..77
Antarctica..78
Chapter 3: Bumps on the Road...80
Homesickness..80
Culture Shock..85
Sexual Harassment...87
Hostel Roommates..91

Traveler's Sick *95*
Chapter 4: Where to Stay **96**
Hotels *96*
Hostels *97*
Airbnb *99*
Homestays *99*
Bed and Breakfast *101*
Chapter 5: Volunteering **102**
Available Opportunities *102*
Websites *105*
Chapter 6: Finding Work **109**
Available Opportunities *109*
How to Find Work *110*
Working Holiday Visas *111*
Teaching English and Certifications *115*
   Visas and Work Permits 116
   Highly Rated Countries to Work In 117
   Teaching Online 121
   Certifications 122
   Dive Master 124
   Au Pair 125
Freelancing *129*
Chapter 7: Returning Home **135**
What to Expect *135*
   "Frozen in Time" 136
   Reverse Culture Shock 137
How to Adjust *138*
   Saving Up Again 139
   Staying in Touch with Friends You Meet 141
Conclusion **142**
About the Expert **143**
Recommended Resources **144**

Introduction

Have you ever told yourself that you were going to travel?

Did you plan to travel after you finished school?

Or, perhaps you needed to take time off from work or school to figure things out.

So why haven't you taken the leap?

What's holding you back?

Do you often say things to yourself such as: "I want to travel, but..."?

If you keep on telling yourself that, you'll never travel and you'll continue to add-on the excuses.

Or, do you say, "I'm waiting for the right person to travel with."

If you're waiting for the "perfect" travel companion, you'll delay traveling even longer. Or never travel because you're too scared to do it alone.

It's time to stop saying "I want to travel, but" or waiting for the "right" person to travel with to come along.

It's time to make a commitment to yourself and work towards your travels.

Let go of every fear you have about solo traveling and just do it! It's empowering, cathartic, and just fun!

You'll meet new and interesting people everywhere you go. Before you know it, you'll have friends from around the world who have your back.

Solo traveling gives you a lot of freedom. You can choose where to go, what to do, and how long to stay in a place.

The best part?

It won't affect someone else.

Traveling also puts you in a situation where it's purely you. There's no right or wrong way to travel solo. Your trip is your trip and should be completely unique to you.

If you want to plan a shorter trip to bigger cities, go for it!

If you want to hitchhike around the globe, also go for it! But, also be safe!

If you find a place you like and want to live there, absolutely do it!

If you want to go on a trip that's between the other options, plan for it!

There's no limit on your travels as long as you are smart and stay safe!

Commit yourself to traveling and make it a priority! If you want it enough, you'll make it happen- no matter what! Don't listen to what other people say about it and stay strong.

After I graduated from university, I traveled around the world solo for six months. This was my first solo trip.

I want to pass on the information I was given before, during, and even after I came home.

I hope by the end of this book or even this introduction, you'll be more confident to take the leap. You won't regret it!

Each chapter will have advice and tips that I was given along with my own personal guidance. A few topics I haven't personally accomplished, but have met handfuls of people who have. I've reached out to them for purposes of this guide.

Let's begin with preparing for your travels!

Chapter 1: Trip Preparation

Planning your trip will be the most time intensive part of your travels!

I'm not talking about planning your daily or even monthly itineraries, which I don't recommend for open-ended traveling.

I'm talking about details you may have overlooked during your initial excitement. This could be visas, budgets, cell phones, etc.

I'll cover all those topics in this chapter and much more! These topics are important to take care of before you leave, especially if your trip is open-ended.

For example, finances are important to take care of before leaving. You wouldn't want to end up in a country, where your ATM and credit card is rejected.

Before I dive into those "business" items, I'll start with one of the most exciting parts of trip preparation: mapping out your travels!

Mapping Your Travels

The first part of your preparation is deciding where you want to start traveling!

Clarifying your starting point gives you a solid goal to work towards. This will also make planning your whole trip easier.

Psychologically, it's easier to say, "I'm going to start my travels in Berlin" rather than, "I'm going to start my travels in Europe."

Start with what continent or region you want to begin your travels in. After, make a list of countries to visit and activities to do. From there, figure out where it makes the most sense to go from your starting point.

For me, I wanted to explore Europe first before going to Asia. I made a list of countries that interested me and what activities I wanted to pursue.

From that list, I figured out where to start and which country to go after. My goal was not to retrace my steps as much as possible. To me, it made the most sense to start my travels in Spain.

I did plan the first month of my travels since I was a little nervous about it.

Looking back, I wish I only planned the first week in Spain and made things up as I traveled through Europe.

There were a couple of places I wished I stayed longer, but since I already bought a bus or train ticket I had to leave.

Having said that, it depends on your comfort level and if you've traveled before globe-trotting solo.

Remember, this is your trip and please do what is most comfortable for you!

Vaccinations

Depending on where your travels take you and where you're from, you may need to get vaccinations.

What vaccinations and types of medicine you may need depend on:

- What countries you plan to travel to.
- What activities you pursue on your travels.
- What vaccinations you've received previously.
- Your current health status.

Diseases such as measles and mumps, now less prevalent in many western countries, are still common in other parts of the world.

Wherever you decide to travel, it's best to consult your doctor if you can! He or she can recommend vaccinations to lower your risk of contracting any disease.

Before I embarked on my travels, I went to see my doctor. There, I asked a few questions:

- Was I up-to-date with my routine vaccinations?
- What vaccinations are advised for my travels?
- Do I need malaria pills?
- Do I need the Yellow Fever vaccination?

Visas

Depending on your passport, you may have travel restrictions! Or, you may need to apply for a visa before arriving in your first country!

Check your home country's government website for any restrictions you may have. It's also a good idea to check that same website for any travel advisory warnings.

I didn't run into many problems in Europe or Asia, but I did need to apply for visas when I traveled throughout Asia.

For example, I needed to fill out a visa application for Nepal. I used the application to receive a visa at the airport when I arrived.

Remember, visa rules vary depending on what passport you hold.

I'll repeat this to emphasize its importance: your country's government website is one of your best resources.

I cannot go through each country's visas rules for you since it would be too much.

Instead, I'll point you towards the right resource.

Budget

One of the biggest questions about travel I get is: How much is it going to cost?

This depends on the length of your trip and what activities you're going to do.

Since you're going around the world, you know it will be longer than three months. Perhaps, you have the intention to travel for a year or longer. Or, maybe you want to travel around and find a place to live.

Whatever your goal may be, you need to research your costs, which will depend on your activities and what type of traveler you are.

Ask yourself:

- Are you backpacking?
- Are you staying in hostels, hotels, or an Airbnb?
- What attractions or sites do you want to see?

After assessing what type of traveler, you want to be, you can piece together an outline of a budget. From there you can figure out how much you are able to spend per day on lodging and food. The bigger expenses would be transportation.

I recommend saving a little more than your budget for emergencies on the road.

Now that you have a loose outline of your budget, you can start saving towards a goal.

Here are a few tips to get started:

- Keep track of all your monthly expenses. You can look at past credit card and bank statements for this. Organize this in an Excel Worksheet or Word Document.
- Determine what expenses you can cut. For example, instead of buying lunch, buy food from the grocery store and make it.
- Spread out any big payments you need to make. This would include doctor and dentist appointments.

Here are a few suggestions to help you save money:

- **Learn to cook and make coffee for yourself**: Both will lower your monthly food bill! And, are useful skills.

- **Roommates:** If you still enjoy living with others, find a roommate or move into a place that needs one. It will cut down on your living expenses and you'll make new friends. If you want and still have the option, you can move back in with your parents.

- **Downgrade your phone plan:** You don't need the latest phone with the most popular phone company. Look for cheaper phone companies that have the same coverage as the popular ones. Some may even let you own your phone instead of renting one.

- **Get a travel rewards credit card:** Look for a credit card that has reward points and starts accumulating them. Down the line, you can use the points to help pay for a plane ticket or buy a gift for yourself.

- **Second-hand Store:** If you must buy new clothes, look for them at second-hand stores. They're far cheaper and you may find unique items there.

- **Sell Your Things:** If you have a pile of unwanted clothes or furniture, just sell it. You won't need it while traveling and putting it into a storage locker is another expense.

- **Don't go to the Movies:** Movies these days are absurdly expensive. You can easily spend up to $20 on tickets and a snack. Rent them from YouTube, Netflix, or iTunes. Spend that $20 on travel!

- **Cut Back on Drinking:** Having a drink with your friends is a nice way to start the weekend, but alcohol is expensive. Drink either before you go out or just don't drink at all.

- **Quit Buying Snacks:** Just as eating out, buying snacks from the vending machine is expensive. You don't think about it since it's only $0.50, but it adds up quickly. Instead, stock up on snacks from the store.

- **Don't Buy Pads and Tampons:** Pads and tampons cost at least $40/month for your period. Instead, buy a menstrual cup. Not only does it save you money it also helps the environment. Keep in mind, if you decide to visit remote places, you won't be able to walk up to the corner store. Plan ahead if you do go to isolated places. If you are able and want to, go on birth control that prevents you from having a period.

While I saved up for my first time around the world, I came home to work and intern during my university breaks.

This also meant I "gave up" taking big trips with my friends. It was hard to see them spending summers with their boyfriends or girlfriends, working an internship in a different city, or road tripping from one end of the country to the other.

In the end, it was worth it since I created an enriching and rewarding trip for myself. Of course, longer than what a university break could offer.

While I am still in the process of saving up for my second world travels, I am doing a lot of the tips I mentioned above.

From my personal experience so far, all the tips work for me! It's hard being on a strict budget, but I know in a year it will all be worth it.

Don't beat yourself up, if you spend too much one weekend, just keep track of your expenses and spend less for the rest of the month.

Cell Phones

While you're traveling, you will need a way to keep in touch with your friends and family!

Of course, your phone is the best way to keep in touch!

But, you don't want to pay a fortune for a phone and an international phone plan.

Instead, buy an unlocked GSM phone and buy SIM cards when you need it.

You'll be able to use all the apps you need when you have access to WIFI.

Keep your phone on airplane mode when you're not using it. This will help save the battery life and allow you to connect with people and your surroundings!

My advice is to limit your phone usage while you're traveling. Be present and snap a few pictures while you're exploring!

You can find a comparable phone to the latest iPhone or Samsung Galaxy for a reasonable price.

Here is a list of the best unlocked phones for under $300:

- **ZTE Axon 7 Mini**
  The ZTE Axon 7 Mini has great hardware along with a budget price of $275. It has a 1.5GHz Snapdragon 617 processor and 3GB of RAM.

You can get up to 32GB of memory to store all your travel photos with room for a microSD card.
What more? You can get up to 15 hours of talk time and have a 50% charge in 30 minutes.

- **Honor 5X**
The Honor 5X is your best bet for a budget phone. It has all the basic smartphone capabilities with a camera that takes photos and videos. This phone allows you to program different fingers to open different apps, which sets it apart from others. The phone has slots that allow for dual microSD, microSIM, and nanoSIM cards. The internal storage is 16GB.

- **Huawei Honor 6X**
The Huawei Honor 6X has the best camera for your budget! You can easily capture the essence of your day and night escapades in faraway lands. Even with such a sophisticated camera, the phone can still last for up to two days before you need to charge it.

- **Moto G Plus (5th Generation)**
The Moto G Plus has the best battery life compared to older models. It can charge up to six hours of use in just 15 minutes. This amazing battery life is due to the Snapdragon CPU that runs so well that it doesn't waste battery life. The screen has beautiful HD visuals and a camera that is comparable to the Huawei Honor 6X.

- **Nokia 6**
  The Nokia 6 has a fast 4g LTE speed, 16 MP camera, and an HD display. It's rated as one of the best budget phones since it's durable. This phone is built with 6000 series anodized aluminum, which gives it an attractive look.

- **LG Q6**
  In a nutshell, the LG Q6 has the quality of a top-notch smartphone without the top-line price tag. LG's Full Vision Tech powers the phone that comes with 3GB of RAM and 32GB of storage. The sides of the phone are made with metal which makes it one of the most durable budget-friendly smartphones.

- **Huawei Ascend Mate 2 Factory Unlocked 4G Phone**
  The Huawei Ascend Mate 2 Factory Unlocked 4G phone isn't the smallest of the budget phones, but it makes reading articles and watching videos more pleasant. This phone comes with 16GB of internal storage with room for up to 32GB with a microSD card.

- **Sony XA1**
  While not the most popular brand, Sony offers unique features only found on their products. This phone can learn your preferences as you figure out how to use it and then optimizes the battery life. The Sony XA1 comes with 16GB of storage and you can add up to 256GB with the SD card slot feature. What really makes this one stand out is the camera. It has 23MP of

resolution to capture all your adventures.

- **Samsung Galaxy J7**
  I know many of you might want the bigger brand names for your smartphone. That's totally fine, but you shouldn't have to spend over $600 for one. The Samsung J7 line is comparable to the S line and you get more for your money. The Samsung Galaxy J7 has the processing power and RAM equal to the latest Android phone. This won't make it seem like a budget phone at all.

What phone you end up choosing ultimately depends on your needs. For me, I needed a phone that had a long battery life, good camera, and was durable.

Before you leave, talk to your phone company about your number. You'll need to use it when you come back. Find out what your options are for keeping your number while on the road.

Travel Apps

There are so many travel apps available to you now. The problem is sorting through all of them and figuring out which ones you need.

Before I left, I talked to many people about which travel apps to use and which ones were just nice to have.

Here is the list of apps I was recommended:

- **Hostelworld**
  This app connects you to all the available hostels in the city you're visiting. It allows you to read reviews, look at photos of the place, and view the different room options. It also has ratings based on value, security, location, staff, atmosphere, cleanliness, and facilities.

- **Rome2Rio**
  This app is one of the best travel apps out there. It's a search engine that tells you how to get from point A to point B. You type in where you are and where you want to go. The results tell you all the options you have to get from point A to point B, along with the price range.

- **Skyscanner**
  This is one of the best flight search engines out there. It does an extensive search when you type in point A and point B. It gives you results from other flight search engines so you don't have to go to different sites.
  The app also tells you which are the cheaper dates to fly out. This is done if you're in calendar view on the app.

- **WhatsApp**
  WhatsApp is a great messaging app that allows you to use your own phone number. With this app, you can connect and keep in touch with people from different countries. Similar to Facebook Messenger, you can call, text, send media, and video chat over WIFI. Not everyone uses the Facebook Messenger app

and this is a great alternative to it.

- **Skype**
  While Skype isn't used as frequently as Facebook Messenger or WhatsApp, it's still good to keep in your arsenal. If you end up volunteering on a farm or hostel, your host may want to Skype with you. After, they'll decide if they want to invite you to come.

- **Couchsurfing**
  Couchsurfing is an app that connects you with local hosts who will let you stay in their house for a couple of nights. You can send requests and message potential hosts through the app. I never used this app and I don't recommend it for solo females. In a different section, I'll discuss why I have this opinion and how to make it safe if you want to pursue the option.

- **Booking.com**
  Booking.com gives you more options to choose from than Hostelworld when you're looking for accommodations. You can choose from hotels, hostels, and even homestays. You can set your budget on the app to help narrow your results.

- **Airbnb**
  Airbnb allows you to stay in a local's space for a price comparable to a nicer hostel. If you find travel companions, you can split the cost. The option might even be cheaper than a hostel with the privacy of a hotel.

- **Maps.Me**
  If you're keeping your phone on airplane mode, you'll need a way to access maps. I used Map.Me as my offline map option. I downloaded the country or region I was going to visit and bookmarked places such as my hostel.

- **Google Translator**
  If you don't have an Android, download Google Translator. Remember, to download the dictionary before you get to your destination! Also, knowing a few phrases in a country's primary language goes a long way with the locals.

I'm confident that if you use these apps, you'll travel smoothly. Of course, if you want to use other apps, then, by all means, download them. Sometimes, I would download apps that were specific to a city I was visiting. After, I uninstalled them from my phone.

Booking Your Flight

Before you skip this section, ask yourself: Have you ever book an international or domestic flight by yourself? Or, do you have a couple booking tricks up your sleeve?

If the answer is "Yes", then skip to a different section.

If the answer is "No", then read or skim through this one.

Believe it or not, there's more to booking a flight than typing in your current location and your destination.

To find the best and cheapest flight follow these tips:

- *If you're set with your final destination and departure date, don't wait to book your flight.* Ticket prices never go down as your departure date approaches. This is especially important if you need to leave on a certain date. Budget airlines in some countries have a base fare and after those seats sell, the price goes up. Your biggest savings will come when you book in advance.

- *Find the Cheapest City to Fly To*
Not every city you want to visit has a big international airport. It's cheaper to fly to a city that does have one. From there, take a bus or train to your final destination. You can even stay a night in a hostel or take a day to explore the city before moving on.

- *Figure Out the Cheapest Day to Fly Out*
You may have heard that booking or flying out on a Tuesday is cheaper. However, that is not always true and the cheapest day to fly is not consistent.
This is where Skyscanner comes in handy! Simply put in what city you're flying out of and into to start. Next, tap the departure date option and select the whole month view.
The whole month view shows you which dates are cheaper to fly out on with a green dot next

to it.

- *Book Your Own Connecting Flights*
  If you're flying somewhere that has a transfer, consider booking the flights separately. Connecting flights often occur when you're making the big leaps between continents or over oceans. Remember, <u>do not book tight layovers.</u> You'll set yourself up for disaster. Play around on Skyscanner and figure out what are the connecting cities and the cheapest way to get to that city.
  Also, do your research on airlines. Look for budget airlines that are specific to the country your flying *out of* and *flying into*.
  Trying this step will save you hundreds of dollars. You can use that for emergencies or something nice while you're traveling.

- *"Hide" Your Search History*
  Airline prices actually do rise after you search a few times on your computer. To combat this, <u>always search for your flights in incognito or private browsing mode.</u>

- *Local Airlines*
  Skyscanner is great for finding cheap flights for bigger airlines such as Asia Air or SouthWest. However, if you're flying to small cities or remote areas, Skyscanner won't be able to give you a flight. Instead, do a Google search and try to find a local airline. If there isn't, just take a bus or train from the biggest city closest to the remote area.

If you follow a few of these tips, I'm sure you'll find the best flight for your trip!

Once you book your flight, it means you're committed to your travels. There's no "undo" button afterward. It's exciting and maybe a little nerve-wracking to new travelers.

Choosing a Hostel

Choosing a hostel is more important than you think, especially for your first stay. You'll want to choose a hostel that is best suited towards your preferences.

Here are a few questions to ask yourself:

- Do I want to be in a social/party environment?
- Do I need a place that accommodates smokers?
- Am I a sensitive sleeper? Can I deal with roommates walking in and out throughout the night?
- Do I need more security because I am traveling with valuables such as a laptop?
- Do I want to stay in a room with all girls or no preference?

Now, that you've figured out what type of hostel you want, search on Hostelworld and Booking.com.

When you're "shopping" for a hostel, here are a few things to keep in mind:

- *Don't go for the cheapest option*
  I know you might be a budget traveler, but think about where that extra money is going. Very cheap hostels, often are not the cleanest or have the best accommodation. Or, sometimes don't pay their staff well. Pay the extra couple of dollars and stay in the second cheapest place. Read the reviews, they'll uncover what the hostel is really like.

- *Choose a Hostel with a Breakfast*
  If you want to have breakfast at the hostel, look for ones that actually have a decent offering. Most hostel's breakfasts (especially in Europe) consist of toast, coffee, and tea. Morning breakfasts are a great place for you to make a snack for yourself and cut back on your food expense. A communal breakfast is also a great place to meet new friends!

- *Late Check- Out/Flexible Check-In Time*
  Try to book a hostel where the checkout time is 10am or later. It's hard to get on the road when you have to wake up early, be quiet around your roommates, and grab your bags in the dark.
  On the other side, hostels that have a flexible check-in time will be a gift! Most hostels don't allow travelers to check-in until 2PM. This is mainly so that they can clean and prepare the rooms, which is understandable. You'll probably be tired after traveling and if you can have a bed right away that would be great. If not, be prepared to sleep in the common room. This shouldn't be a make or break aspect, but

really something to be aware of for hostel policies.

- *Lockers and Security*
  If high security and lockers are important for you, make sure the hostel upholds these standards! You want to make sure there's good security throughout the hostel. Having lockers in your dorm room is a huge plus. You can bring your own lock or rent one from the hostel. This is a deal breaker for most people since they don't want to worry about their valuables while exploring the city.

- *Common Area*
  One of the reasons you picked a hostel is to meet new people! Besides your hostel roommates, the next place to make friends is in the common area. A hostel that gives its travelers a place to hang out, meet, and socialize is a good one. This makes it easier for solo travelers to make friends. My best advice is to stick yourself in a common area, get off your phone, and start talking with the person next to you.

- *Hostel Organized Activities*
  Really good hostels organize activities such as walking tours, family dinners, bar crawls, and similar activities. This would be something to look for as a female solo traveler. You know you'll be in a safe environment and be able to meet new friends! This shouldn't be a make or break consideration. I've met some of my

friends in common areas or my hostel dorm.

- *Staff Members*
  The staff members can really make a difference for your hostel stay. Read the reviews and look for hostels that have a knowledgeable and friendly staff. Remember, you want to feel welcomed in a hostel and be able to ask a staff member for advice or if you're having a problem.

Be sure to read through the hostel reviews when you're "shopping" around. They are your best tool when it comes to picking the hostel for you! Try to stay at hostels with consistent and positive reviews.

Health Insurance

Health insurance for travelers is different than traveler's insurance, which I'll discuss in the next section.

Health insurance is always a tough call.

If you're young, healthy, and tend to stay out of trouble, you'll probably be fine without it.

Having said that, if something does happen, your home country's insurance may not be accepted.

Or, worst case, the medical staff discovers you're from a western country without health insurance and might try to make you pay more. The only place this might happen is in Asia and only in certain situations. Not if you have to go to the pharmacy.

I'd recommend getting health insurance specifically for travelers. Shop around for plans that would cover you in the event of an emergency. The plan should offer basic medical benefits if you break a bone or catch a virus.

Since you'll be traveling for an extended period of time, look for *high deductible* health insurance plans that cover emergencies only.

If you're not sure where to start, here is a list of different companies.

- *Cigna Global Health Insurance*
  Cigna Global Health is one of the oldest health insurance providers. The company tailors towards expatriates and offers a range of global medical insurance plans. Cigna has world-wide medical coverage that has the option to include the United States.

- *Allianz*
  Allianz covers trips that last up to a year and can insure up to $1 million. Some plans will pay back up to 150% of your trip if it's ended early due to medical problems.

- *IMG Global*
  IMG Global offers plans up to two years' worth of coverage. Plans are offered to all types and ages of travelers. For example, the company covers a policy if you're 65 and older with a

pre-existing condition that "suddenly" comes back.

- *AIG Travel Guard*
  AIG Travel Guard offers three levels of protection from basic to comprehensive. A basic plan would include common travel-related issues such as a sore throat. While a comprehensive one would include medical emergencies and evacuations.

- *World Nomads*
  World Nomads is a company for the adventurers out there. Plans can include sports such as trekking, glacier hiking, surfing, skydiving, etc. This company caters towards independent travelers so plans can be extended once they've started.

Please do your own research and find the best company and plan for you! This list was merely to help start your search.

Traveler's Insurance

Traveler's insurance covers travel "bumps" such as lost luggage, flight cancellations, other losses during the trip, and sometimes medical insurance.

Unlike medical insurance, this type typically is geared more towards travel related issues, as mentioned above.

This type of insurance is better for trips that have a definitive starting and stopping point. If this is the type of trip you're planning for, then look into traveler's insurance. However, I don't think it's necessary even for short trips.

For those of you who are planning for an open-ended trip, traveler's insurance is something you can definitely opt-out.

Many of the companies listed in the previous section, also offer traveler's insurance.

If you're not sure where to start, here is a short list of the top-rated companies:

- *Allianz Global Assistance*
  Allianz Global Assistance is a huge company, which means it can offer more types of plans, more coverage, and at a lower rate. The company works fast on claims and quickly resolves any glitches.

- *Amex Assurance*
  Amex Assurance is associated with American Express, but you don't have to be a cardholder to receive the benefits! Amex offers a variety of coverage and insurance policies depending on your trip.

- *Seven Corners*
  Seven Corners is a privately-owned insurance company, that also offers traveler's health insurance. It's a company that deals with many

American and foreign companies so it's quite attuned to what a traveler may need.

Credit and Debit Cards

Credit cards are used to pay for almost everything we buy now from groceries and gas to plane and train tickets.

Now, there are hundreds of credit cards and deals to select from. With the number of cards available it's hard to pinpoint which ones are the best for travelers and which ones are scams.

It can be tricky to get through all the sign-up perks, loyalty programs, and the dreaded hidden fees.

Most people are not willing to sort through all of it and just use a debit card.

Stop yourself, if you're that person. Using your debit card for all purchases is a terrible idea. If someone makes a purchase with your debit card, your money is gone for good. If the same situation happens with a credit card, you can dispute the charges.

Credit cards can reward you for your current spending habits.

In this section, I'll tell you how to choose the travel credit card that suits you.

Remember, travel credit cards let you earn reward points through your spending. Later, you can use those reward points towards airfare, hotel rooms, or a special excursion!

As I'm saving up for my next trip, I'm also accumulating my travel reward points on my credit card.

The next question is, how do you select the best travel credit card for you?

Let's start with stage one.

Stage One: Define Your Goal

Your "perfect" card depends on your goals and possibly spending habits. So, don't worry about what card someone else is using!

To begin, define your goal.

Do you want a brand loyalty card? Or, are you more concerned about reward points and no fees?

What type of perks do you want from a card? Elite status?

How do you want to use your reward points? As cash or to help pay for a plane ticket?

For example, if you're a frequent flyer of United Airlines, then sign up for their card and rack up miles!

Do you want to "earn" a free hotel room? Look into hotels that have a partnership with a credit card company!

When you define your goal, search for a card that will help you reach it and match your spending habits. From there, you'll be able to use your travel credit card to your advantage.

Stage Two: Important Aspects to Look for in a Travel Credit Card

- *Reward Point Sign-On Bonus*
  A sign-on bonus is what helps you accumulate reward points easily. This usually happens if you meet the minimum spending requirement within a specific number of days.

- *Additional Categories to Earn Travel Reward Points*
  Most good travel credit cards let you earn one point for every dollar spent. However, great travel credit cards allow you to earn more points when you shop at specific stores. This will help you rack-up those points even more quickly!

- *Special Benefits*
  Nearly all travel credit cards have special benefits for them. For example, many will not have foreign transaction fees. Other benefits may include priority boarding or a free night at a hotel. Think about what other benefits you want from the card other than the reward

points.

- *No Annual Fees*
  Many travel credit cards, which have an annual fee, also happen to be the ones with the best reward plans. If you're a budget traveler, I'd stay clear of those types of cards. If you're a frequent traveler with a more money to spend, then a card with a fee could be worth it.

- *No Foreign Transaction Fee*
  Look for credit cards that don't have a foreign transaction fee! What good is having a card that charges you a fee every time you use it abroad?

Not all of the aspects will be on every travel credit card. Just choose the card that has a few of them. For me, I needed a card that let me earn points without the foreign transaction and annual fees.

As for debit cards, you will need to take one with you so you can withdraw cash from the ATM. Look for a bank that has very low foreign transactions fees and ATM fees. Those can accumulate quickly if you're going to the ATM frequently. My advice is to take the maximum amount of money you think you need. That way, you're not charged fees every two days.

Staying in Touch with Friends and Family

Staying in touch with your friends and family might be one of the most important things.

If something happens to you, your family will at least know the last place you've been. They can contact the hostel or wherever you're staying to ask about you.

Let your parents know where you're headed next and how you're getting there. Forward your plane, bus, or train ticket itinerary. Every little thing helps them stay calm while you're out there.

Checking-in with your parents just lets them know you're doing ok and you don't need their help just yet.

Since you'll be traveling with an unlocked phone, pick <u>one</u> way to keep in touch whether that be Facebook Messenger, WhatsApp, or Skype.

For friends, I'd suggest keeping in touch with maybe five at most. It's hard to keep up with all of them. It's truly best just to pick the five you feel closest to. The others will understand that traveling makes you tired and you can't always give the most detail over text or call time. The time difference also makes it difficult to have "regular" contact.

For my trip, I kept in touch with my parents and a few friends while I was gone. The people who I did not regularly keep in touch with still were my friends when I came back and wanted to hear about my travels and plans for the future.

Boyfriends and Girlfriends

If you have a boyfriend or girlfriend, I recommend just breaking it off with him or her.

I know it's a tough decision to go through, but you'll be better off.

This tip is especially important if your trip is open-ended. Your boyfriend or girlfriend won't have to continually hope that the next flight you book is back to them. And, you won't feel obligated to return because someone misses you.

Your travels will change you so much; you'll have different goals and a new "identity" to immerse yourself in.

Believe it or not, after traveling your current boyfriend or girlfriend might not be the person for you. Going back to them, would be like going back in time. It seems like it would be nice to visit the past. But, you realize that it wasn't what you remembered and not in a good way. You will have changed and they won't. They can't support the new you.

If things do work out for you two when you return home, then I applaud you! It's great! Tell me how you two worked it out.

If you have a definitive start and end point to your travels, then it might make sense to keep in touch. Of course, this varies from couple to couple. Have an open discussion with your partner to work something out.

Luggage

Luggage is one of the most crucial purchases you'll make for your trip. Remember, this bag needs to last you for a long time and you can't get tired of carrying it around.

You'll need something durable, light, and be able to hold what you end up packing.

In addition to your backpack, you'll need some type of day bag that you can take exploring with you.

To start, let's discuss the different types of backpacks available to you!

All of the ones listed below can be carried on and are not backpacker backpacks, which are too big. You'll get tired of carrying a huge bag after a few hours at the airport.

You'll be glad you took one the ones listed below:

- **Osprey FarePoint and FairView**
  Osprey is a popular travel backpack for its durability and lightness. These backpack models offer the features of a backpacker's backpack in a smaller version. It comes in 40L, 55 L, and 70L sizes. Just pick which size is best suited for your travels.

- **Osprey Porter**
  Similar to the Osprey listed above, this one is a little more basic in terms of features, but still comfortable and well-made to last throughout

your travels. This one comes in 30 L, 46L, and 65L. This backpack comes with hips straps to help relieve your shoulders.

- **Tortuga Outbreaker Travel Backpack**
  Tortuga has a panel-look that is made of durable material with a padded hip belt. The suspension system is well designed with a traveler in mind with padded shoulder straps. This bag comes in two sizes: 35L and 45L.

- **AER Travel Pack**
  AER Travel Pack is specifically created for the urban traveler. It has a slim and sleek look to it with many pockets to stick your personal items in.

For day bags, research ones that can be kept close to your body and can hold your daily supplies. You shouldn't bring more than your phone and wallet with you around town. Maybe a book or journal if you're feeling it that day.

Packing

While packing for an open-ended trip around the world seems complicated, it's really not.

You won't need more than a week's worth of clothes along with your toiletries and passport, and journal if you'd like. Trust me, you'll get tired of lugging around half your closet after day one.

Here is a suggested packing list:

- One pair of "heavy" pants to wear on the plane.
- One "heavy" or long-sleeved shirt to wear on the plane.
- One pair of "light" pants to wear around the town.
- One pair of shorts.
- 1-2 tank tops
- 1-2 shirts
- Raincoat
- Light Jacket
- One nice outfit (skirt and a nice shirt or one dress)
- Enough underwear for a week
- 1-2 sports bras and one regular bra
- 3 pairs of socks
- 2 pairs of shoes (a "heavier pair" and a pair of sandals)
- Bathing suit, if you already have one
- Water bottle
- Toiletries
- Adapter for your electronics
- Birth control, especially if you take oral contraceptives

While you're packing, don't forget to make copies of your financial information and passport! Tuck those copies in a couple safe spots in your bag. And, give a copy to your parents or whoever is your trusted person.

Remember, you're not out in the middle of nowhere, you can buy new clothes if you need to. I actually ended up sending home clothes I was barely wearing.

To make your clothes last longer, wash some in the sink if you need to. Take clothes that can easily be mixed and matched. Other travelers live out their backpacks and will repeat outfits so you can too!

The list is just suggestive, if you want to take more, then go ahead! Do what is best for you and your travel style and trip!

Birth Control

Birth control might be something overlooked during the excitement of trip preparation.

If you take oral contraceptives, this section is for you!

Those of you, who have an IUD implant, or not on any birth control then you can skip this section. Fortunately, the IUD and implant will last throughout your open-ended travels. You also have the option to get it replaced or removed while you're traveling.

For those of you on the pill, talk to your doctor before you leave. Tell her the nature of your trip especially if it's open-ended.

From there, talk about what your options are. You might want to switch methods or stay on the pill if that's what you are more comfortable with.

If you stay on the pill, ask if your doctor can write a script that can last up to two years. Try to buy as many packs of pills as you can before you leave. And of course, keep your prescription and a copy of it.

To make sure everything goes smoothly, concerning your birth control, make sure you plan far in advance. This is gravely important if you switch methods since you'll need "test" it out.

Chapter 2: How to Stay Safe

One of the most common concerns you'll have is how to stay safe.

Perhaps you're worried that being alone will make you an easy target or you've heard bad news about female solo travelers.

Forget all your preconceived notions about the dangers of traveling alone!

Yes, there are skills needed to keep yourself safe, but they aren't any different than the ones you use back home.

How do you keep yourself safe?

Trust your intuition and gut feeling. If something doesn't seem right get out of the situation quickly. Locals are more likely to help or talk to you since you'll be alone. It's easier for them to approach a solo traveler rather than a group of travelers.

In this chapter, I'll discuss general safety tips along with other topics relevant to women.

I'll also talk about situations you should just avoid altogether. Although if you really want to pursue those, I'll tell you how to do it as safely a possible.

General Safety Tips

After reading the last section, do you feel that you already have the skills to stay safe?

If not, here is a short list of tips I knew previously to leaving and learned along the way.

- *Trust Your First Thoughts*
  Best advice is to trust your intuition about any situation you run into. If something doesn't feel right or if someone is giving off a weird vibe, get yourself out of there. Do it sooner rather than later. A bad feeling leads to a horrible situation fast.

- *Just Say "No"*
  Your solo travels are supposed to be on your own terms so don't be afraid to say "no" to anything or anybody.
  Some bars and hostels encourage the group to keep drinking or go to the bars every time you go out.
  You'll earn respect for saying no to that extra drink and defining your boundaries.
  You want to remember what you did on your trip and you can't do that if you black out every other night.

- *Keep Valuables Close*
  Keep your valuables close to you. Find a day bag that allows you to have your wallet, phone, and possibly passport closest to you. It's easy to lose track of valuables if they aren't with you all

the time.

- *Talk to the Locals*
Ask the locals or staff at your hostel what to look out for while you're exploring the city. Some cities are notorious for pickpockets and scammers who target tourists. It's better to ask rather than the alternative.

- *Follow the "Dress Code"*
Do your research and dress appropriately for whatever country you're visiting. When you stick out in the crowd, you become an easy target for thieves and sexual harassers. Unfortunately, you can't always wear what you want in hot weather such as short shorts and tank tops. If you packed a dress with you, it will make walking around the tropical countries more bearable.

- *Don't Walk Alone at Night*
This tip is one you probably practice frequently at home! And, applies to anywhere you find yourself. Sometimes, this situation is hard to avoid. If you do walk alone at night, stick to the main streets, have a map in your head. And, if you need to look at your phone, walk into a convenience store.

- *Copy Your Sensitive Documents*
Make copies of your sensitive documents such as your passport, credit card information, and health insurance.
Make a copy for yourself and keep it safe in your bag.

Make another copy for your parents or whoever your trusted person is.

- *Know the Emergency Numbers*
Research what the emergency numbers are for the country you're visiting. If you're really nervous, also bookmark the nearest hospital on your online and offline map.

- *Keep Your Parents and Friends in the Loop*
Send your parents and a trusted friend your travel information. This would include where you're going, where you're staying, and how you're getting there. For example, I told my parents the hostel I was going to and about what time I'd arrive there. If I was flying, I'd forward my itinerary to them.

Do any of these tips seem new to you?

I bet not! You're probably already masters of all these skills and more.

You'll have no problem traveling solo after reading those reminders.

Couchsurfing

Couchsurfing is one of those situations you should avoid at all costs.

It seems like a fun and cheap way to travel and explore the town with a local.

However, this is one of the most dangerous scenarios and puts you in a very compromising position. Once you're in your host's house, you're at their will. You can't predict his or her ulterior motive or how they act in-person.

Anyone can act the part as a caring or "perfect host" online.

The Couchsurfing community used to be more tight-knit and a safe space when it was founded. After the company was sold to a for-profit company, in 2011, it became a place for perverts.

A lot of guys look here to find a quick hook-up from solo female travelers. Instead of providing a safe place to rest for a couple days, which was the original goal of the site.

If that's how you want to travel, then do whatever you want-it's your trip. No one will think little of you because of it-trust me! Just be safe!

There are many stories of girls, who find a good host online. However, when they meet in-person, their hosts don't act or follow through with whatever guidelines they agreed to online. Worst case, they are raped or end up dead.

Supposedly, you're staying at someone's place for free and they're expecting nothing in return. For guys, what they want in return is to sleep or have sex with you.

If you want to pursue this option, try these tips to make it "safe":

- *Read the Reviews*
  Don't just read what the reviews say but who leaves the reviews. If a host's profile is full of girls then that should raise a flag.

- *Couchsurf with Female Hosts*
  It might be "safer" to stay with female hosts instead of male ones. This doesn't automatically put you in the green light just because you have a female host. Message them and read their profile. If you see any red flag signs, just don't do it.

- *Define What You're Looking For*
  Be extremely clear in your message correspondence that you're only looking for a place to rest. Make sure your profile matches this and be clear that you're not using Couchsurfing as a dating or hookup service.

- *Backup Accommodation*
  If you end up Couchsurfing, make sure you have another place to stay. There are countless stories of girls meeting their hosts and then deciding "no". If this happens to you, have a hostel or hotel in mind.

Hitchhiking

Hitchhiking is another situation you should avoid at all costs.

It may seem fun and of course a free way to travel from place to place.

However, this puts you in another compromising situation.

Your driver may not take you where you want to go or sexually harass you. This can be hard to escape if the car is going really fast or you fall asleep during the ride.

If you wish to try hitchhiking, try these tips:

- *Listen to Your Instincts*
  If you end up getting a ride and you feel uneasy, ask to be dropped off ASAP. Even if it's in the middle of nowhere. You'll be much better off than staying in the car. That uneasy feeling can turn sour in a matter of seconds.

- *Ask for a Ride*
  Go to petrol or gas stations instead of standing at the side of the road. You have more choices of drivers that way. You can "interview" drivers. Never say where you're going first, ask where the driver is going and then ask if you can ride along. If the driver seems unreliable, then you can pretend you're not going the same way.

- *Truck Drivers*
  Truck drivers can be a "safe" bet when you're looking for a driver. Truckers have to give their company details of their routes and must pass specific checkpoints.

- *Take Action*
  If you end up taking a ride and then fall into danger, take action! Flail your arms out of the windows to get another driver's attention. Open the car door. Reach over to the driver's wheel and pull it to show that you're not going to be pushed around.

As I've mentioned before, this is your trip and travel on your terms. If you wish to hitchhike or Couchsurf, please be careful and do more research before leaping into it!

Travel Companions

Of course, part of the reason you travel is to meet new and interesting people! And, believe me, you'll meet new friends everywhere you go!

If you meet a traveler-either male or female- who you really get along with, you two may decide to travel together!

That would be great if that happened! It would definitely make your travelers safer, easier, and possibly cheaper.

Unlike traveling with a boyfriend or girlfriend, there is an understanding you don't have to do everything together. You can do different activities and split off at any time. There are no hard feelings when you part and you can stay in touch! Who knows, you may run into him or her again.

When you do find a person to travel with, there should be a couple things you agree on.

Here are the suggested topics to discuss:

- How long do you want to travel together?
- How much time do you want to spend together?
- Determine a loose route.
- Discuss if you're splitting costs.

As I mentioned before, your travel companion doesn't have to be female. There are advantages to traveling with a guy rather than a group of girls.

Here are a few advantages of traveling with a guy:

- An extra layer of "security" when you're out at night or even walking around during the day.
- Fewer sexual harassment situations. People may mistake you two as a couple and some guys will back off.
- A different perspective on a situation. Guys' brains work differently and they may pick up on something you didn't realize! This can be a good and bad detail that can make a big difference.

Here are a few things to look for in a travel companion:

- *Have a Shared Interest*
  Remember, you're looking for a travel companion, not someone to date unless that's what you want. Try to find someone who has a few shared interests as you do. You won't spend all your time together so it's ok if you don't have a "perfect" match.

- *Stay Clear of "High Maintenance" Travelers*
  "High maintenance" means different things to different travelers. If there's something you can't put up with, then don't travel with him or her. Remember, it could be something such as sleeping-in too late, drinking too much, packing heavy, or has dietary restrictions. Know your limits and keep that in mind.

- *Agree to a Budget*
  Your budgets do not have to match, but they do need to be similar. Doing so ensures that you guys will have a positive traveling experience! Your budget affects nearly every aspect of travel: where you stay, where you go, what you do, and how to get between towns.

- *Communication*
  Make sure you and your travel companion can communicate! Before you start traveling, have a conversation about a budget, dealing with problems, and how you each picture your travels. Do you picture you two doing everything together or just a few things? Once

you decide to travel together, try to create a few ground rules.

Of all the tips above, I'd say one of the most important is communication. Without it, the whole experience won't be what either of you two wanted.

Again, don't worry if you don't find a travel companion.

I never traveled with anyone else; just met people wherever I went. Not a lot of people were going the same way as me. It didn't lessen my traveling experience at all! It made it more liberating since it was all on my own terms.

"Safer" Countries

Are you committed to traveling?

Are you nervous about which country to visit?

If you answered "yes" to both these questions, then feel free to read this chapter.

I understand that being out on your own can be nerve-racking to some.

I created this chapter to help ease you into solo traveling.

Maybe you want to start your worldly travels in a "safer" country before moving on.

There's nothing wrong with starting your travels where you feel the most *comfortable*. It might make traveling seem less intimating and make you travel even longer!

These "safer" countries are accustomed to thousands of tourists coming through every year. You might even experience less culture shock if you get any at all.

For this section, I've compiled a list of "safe" countries in different regions throughout the world.

No matter what region you start in, these lists should help you plan the first part of your travels!

Please don't feel limited to what countries I mention below! It's a suggested starting point and I can't suggest the best country without knowing your preferences.

The best thing you can do is look up countries based on your interests. Or, research what activities you can do in countries you might like to visit.

Europe

- *Iceland*
  Iceland is one of the best places to travel as a female solo traveler!
  Why?
  It's a popular country so you'll meet new people at every corner you turn!
  If you're a city or nature lover or even both, you'll find things to do. You can go hiking in the many national parks, or wander around the city.
  The capital city, Reykjavik, is very easy to navigate once you're there.
  The burgeoning music and nightlife scenes create opportunities to connect with people you meet in the hostels or the locals.
  Even if you find yourself outside of major cities, the locals are very friendly and the rate of crime is extremely low.

- *Netherlands*
  The Netherlands is a great place to start too! Especially if you're wandering in Amsterdam, Netherlands. The whole city has a laid-back and liberal vibe and also bike-friendly. You can

explore the city on a budget and work out your legs and butt! The city is very attuned to different types of travelers. This means you can meet people from different walks of life as you explore!

- *Scotland*
  Scotland also has a good rating in terms of safety in nearly every city. The most top rated for travelers is Edinburgh! If you're scared of the language difference, no need to worry here. Almost everyone speaks English.
  Only here, can you fulfill your wanderlust-ness for both ancient relics and dancing to the newest local music!

- *Slovenia*
  If you want to explore eastern Europe, but are nervous, try starting with Slovenia. Eastern Europe often gets a bad rapport for its supposedly "dangerous" cities.
  Go to Ljubljana, to start since it can easily be accessed by train or plane. It's also safe and not as traveled compared to other cities. This means you'll be able to discover a different part of Europe and push slightly out of your comfort zone. The city is cheaper compared to other countries and laid back!

- *Spain*
  Spain is one of the top travel destinations around! Doesn't matter if you're a solo traveler or in a group.
  Start in Barcelona! The city has everything you could want: fascinating sites, great beach

weather, bubbling culture, and exciting flavors to try! You can experience all of that with very low risks for sexual harassment, theft, etc.

- *Ireland*
  Ireland is one of the most laid back and humble countries to start your world travels in. Dublin hosts many pubs, museums, and live music to sink your teeth into. All places you can create shared memories with the people you meet. The country also offers recreational activities. You can trek and take long hikes through rolling hills and those famous cliff-hanging seashores.

- *Czech Republic*
  Before you explore other parts of Czech Republic, I strongly suggest you start in Prague. You can wander around that city for hours alone and find new and fascinating wonders. You'll run into churches, museums, gardens, and other sites at every turn. The locals are used to travelers and are more than happy to help or give you suggestions.

- *Germany*
  Germany is famous for Berlin and its many castles around the country. Of course, Berlin is a great place to visit for its multi-cultural vibe and to see The Berlin Wall.
  However, if you want to seek out a "break" from the current world, visit Rothenburg ob der Tauber. The city is stuck in the Medieval Ages in terms of its architecture and cobblestone roads. The city's beauty draws tourists to

it every year making it a traveler-friendly city!

- *France*
  Nearly everyone wants to visit Paris and there's no reason not to go! With the number of travelers that come through, you'll meet new people every day. It houses the Louvre and other amazing sites such as the Eiffel Tower. It has amazing street-side cafes, where you can people watch or gaze at the architecture while reading or journaling.
  If you're more of a beach person, southern France is amazing in the summertime!

- *Hungary*
  Begin your travels in Hungary with Budapest! It's very budget-friendly while offering high-end hostels, one-of-a-kind local food, and ancient castles.
  While you're in Budapest, make sure to check out one of the thermal bath spas! They're affordable and truly an experience you'll only find in Budapest.

Middle East

While the Middle East is a part of Asia, I decided to dedicate a section to the region. It is vastly different than eastern Asia and thought it best write separates sections.

- *Northern Palestine and Israel*
  Go to Northern Palestine and Israel to

experience the complications and allure of the Middle East.

In Northern Palestine, try starting in either Nablus, Ramallah, or Bethlehem. In those cities, you can safely explore the Holy Land, which has a mix of Christian history, Palestinian food, and Middle Eastern friendliness.

In Israel, I suggest starting in either Nazareth, Haifa, or Jerusalem. All the cities will provide you with a rich historical background in a stunning setting.

- *Qatar*
  Don't let Qatar's uneasy relationship with its gulf neighbors fool you. This country is extremely safe to travel solo. The citizens of the country support their government so you won't have to worry about protests or marches.
  Once you decide to start in Qatar, you have a few options on hand. You can begin exploring Doha, the lively and social capital city, or one of the coastal cities, where you can swim in the Arabian Sea. All over, you can experience the Qatari food which is famous for its spices and cinnamon.

- *United Arab Emirates*
  The United Arab Emirates hosts millions of tourists every year, which makes it one of the safest countries to travel solo. You'll meet plenty of people to explore the dazzling cities such as Dubai or Abu Dhabi.
  Dubai is home to the world's biggest mall and tallest building along with other "world's" best

sites to gaze at.
No matter which city you go to, you'll experience a wonderful mix of splendor, long-established customs, cosmopolitan scene, local flavor, and of course new and interesting food to try.

- *Oman*
  Oman, a quiet and unassertive country, once "hidden" from tourists, now is becoming more popular among travelers. Go here, before this whole country becomes flooded with tourists. Only here, you'll see spectacular nature and warming hospitality from the locals. The coastline cities are breath-taking with some of the best river valleys (wadis) to visit.
  Overall, this country has one of the lowest crime rates in the world making it ideal for solo female travelers.

- *Jordan*
  Jordan is a safe country to visit because it doesn't have any political problems and has high stability.
  Explore the alluring capital city, Amman, and immerse yourself in the fascinating history in Petra.
  No matter what type of traveler you are, there is an activity for everyone. You can explore one of the country's famous deserts, walk through history in the Roman ruins, or get lost in nature in the Wadi Rum.

- *Egypt*
  Even though parts of Egypt such as Cairo and

the Sinai Peninsula have occasional terror attacks, the northern part of the country and Alexandria is safe.
Enjoy Alexandria since it is famous for being influenced by French, Greek, and Jewish cultures. Alexandria is a hub for a lot of tourists in Egypt.
Go to the northern coastline and take a dip in the Mediterranean Sea.
No trip to Egypt isn't complete until you visit the Giant Pyramids, of course!

- *Kuwait*
  In the massive Arabian Peninsula, Kuwait occupies a small corner of it.
  Kuwait is well-known for being a country for expats and immigrants in the Middle East.
  Kuwait City, the capital of the country, is home to a variety of exciting mosques, bazaars, and shop stalls.

Asia

- *Cambodia*
  Cambodia is full of rich history and culture, which has made it a destination for female solo travelers from around the world.
  Here, you can explore and admire the beauty and greatness of Angkor Wat; take a refreshing dip in Sihanoukville beach, and; learn about Khmer culture and food! These are just a few activities you can start with!
  Phnom Penh is a great place to learn about

history. Not far from this city, are the killings fields and genocide museum. You'll learn who the Khmer Rouge is and what they did. It will be a valuable history lesson you don't want to skip out on.

- *Thailand*
  In Thailand, you can find stunningly beautiful white-sanded beaches, majestic mountains, and spicy Thai food to try!
  Bangkok is a dynamic, hot city you can explore. It has the stunning Wat Arun Temple, a Chinatown Market, and a party scene at the Khao San and RCA.
  For a more laid back and country-feel, travel to Chiang Mai in northern Thailand. There, you'll find temples, mountains, and other outdoor adventures. The Loi Kathrong festival is the best experience in this city because of its intimate setting on the river.
  Pai is another city to visit after Chiang Mai and where you can easily stay a month.

- *Vietnam*
  Vietnam is a country, where you'll run into the same people again and again. Many people travel from either north to south or south to north on scooters.
  While you're traveling through Vietnam you can visit the country's beaches, rivers, and Buddhist Pagodas.
  You'll be able to walk through Vietnam's history if you look closely at the architecture, which has been influenced throughout the years.

Use Hanoi as a "home base" once you get to northern Vietnam. Take trips to Sapa for a trek through the rice fields or to Halong Bay to do a day cruise with your new friends.

- *Malaysia*
  Malaysia has something for every female solo traveler out there. You can choose from island escapades, cityscapes, and rolling nature.
  To fulfill your island wanderlust, try starting on either Sipadan, Pulau Redang, or Tioman islands. There, you can soak up the sun, go for a dip or even go snorkeling.
  Kula Lumpur is home to Petronas Towers, which will fulfill your big-city dreams.
  Take-in the unique nature at Gunung National Park, Batu Caves, or the Cameron Highlands.
  If you want to have a more immersive cultural experience, look for a homestay in Sarawak Cultural Village or similar ones.

- *Japan*
  Compared to the South East Asian countries, Japan is another continent.
  Tokyo is full of fun at every corner. Whether you're looking for the latest high-tech video game bar or a modern, forward-moving city, you'll find it in this country.
  If you want to go to an urban, but not too fast-paced city, take the bullet train to visit Osaka and Kyoto. In Kyoto, you can see the famous cherry blossom trees.
  This city also gives you the "old spirit" of the country with its many shrines such as Fushimi Inari-Taisha and Arashiyama.

Japan won't be as cheap as some other Asian countries, but don't let that deter you from visiting this lovely country. You can figure out how to visit everything on your list with your budget.

- *Laos*
  Laos is another country you can fit into a loop between Thailand, Cambodia, and Vietnam. In Laos, you can escape from the busy urban life of Vietnam and parts of Thailand. You can find peace and culture wrapped together wherever you wander in this country.
  Visit Wat Xieng Tong, the country's most popular monastery, where you can observe peace and meditation at its best.
  Looking for an eco-friendly, trip? Book a visit to the Bokeo Nature Reserve Wilderness.
  Laos also offers small treks intertwined with cultural immersion in Phongsali and Luang Prabang.

- *Nepal*
  Nepal is one for the true adventurers out there. Nepal is the place you can go trekking for up to three weeks. On treks, you'll walk nearly six hours a day until you are surrounded by the majestic, breathtaking mountains.
  This country connects adventure seekers through the trekking industry. Trekkers meet each other in hostels or on the trek.
  You'll be able to come alone and walk away with a few friends.

- *Indonesia*
  Indonesia is made up a chain of islands across South East Asia's region.
  Take in the spectacularly alluring views of the Arjuna-Welirang volcanoes, gaze at Candi Sukuh temple in Java, or be amazed in Tana Toraja's boat houses.
  If you're a beach girl, just go to Bali and relax there.

- *China*
  China might be the first country that comes to mind when you hear "Asia", which is why I didn't list it first. I'm not downplaying the wonderful cities and sites the country has to offer. I wanted to highlight the other amazing options you have in Asia.
  China has the Great Wall of China, Forbidden City, and the Temple of Heaven as "classic" sites you can see.
  This country is huge so research what is there!

- *Philippines*
  The Philippines is a great place for female solo travelers since the locals are innately optimistic and welcoming.
  This is another country for the outdoorsy women out there.
  Throughout the country, you can find places where you can swim, dive, surf or snorkel. Siargao is a spot for the surfers; Tubbataha Reef for the divers and snorkelers, and the many beaches for the swimmers.

- *Singapore*
  If you can't choose from any of the Asian countries on your personal list or this one, then go to Singapore. The country converges many Asian cultures into one country.
  The crime rate is extremely low which allows you to explore sites from the Marina Bay Sands; cultural districts such as Little Arab, Little India, and China town.

- *India*
  Don't let the news spoil your opinions of India. This country is relatively safe as long as you use the same safety skills we discussed earlier.
  See the famous Taj Mahal in the north and then venture down south for a different culture, hospitality, and food!
  There's so much to do in India, I could dedicate another guide to it! Research what's there based on your interests.

North America

- *United States of America*
  The United States of America is a huge country with so much to see and do! The landscape changes from deciduous forests to deserts and to beaches.
  There's everything from preserved nature in one of the many national parks to big bustling hub cities such as New York City, Chicago, Seattle, and Los Angeles.
  I suggest starting on one of the coastal cities

such as New York, Boston, Seattle, or Los Angeles, since those bring in the most tourists each year. You can meet people and then decide to head east or west into the country. Want to go to a smaller town?
I recommend trying to stay with a family. You can get a taste of a local's life and learn new skills if you're doing a homestay or farmstay.

- *Canada*
  Canada, the United States' neighbor, also has a wide variety of activities to do. The east and west coast of the country vary drastically in landscape and cityscape just as its neighbor. Vancouver has many great parks to choose from outside the city, where you can fulfill your outdoor adventure lust. The city itself is huge and has a great public transportation system get you from site to site.
  Use Halifax, Nova Scotia as your "base" city. Plan day trips with all your new friends to places such as Peggy's Point Lighthouse.
  Toronto is a big city with many things to do and a very friendly city as well. There are sites such as Kensington Market and the Distillery District to explore.
  Want a taste of Europe?
  Go to Quebec, where you'll feel as if you're exploring the streets of Europe! Be sure to visit at least one of these places: Old Montreal, Mont-Royal, Parc Jean Drapeau, and Montreal Biodome.

Central America

- *Mexico*
  Start in Mexico City to brush up on your history. There are many museums that can give you a different perspective on history. From there, go to Chichen Itza, where the country's most famous Mayan temple is located. You'll be blown away from its beauty and the pure fact that it has survived for so long.
  If you are a nightlife person, plan a few nights in Cancun and the Rivera Maya. You'll be able to relax on the beaches or cenotes during the day and grab a drink in the evening.

- *Belize*
  Belize is the only English-speaking country in Central America since it was a British colony. This country is overflowing with diversity. If you're a water person spend as much time as you want in Cayes or Caribbean Islands or the Great Blue Hole. You can explore the waters by snorkeling or scuba diving.
  For the jungle explorers, head inland for guided tours to catch a glimpse at a big cat or go caving.

- *Guatemala*
  Guatemala has a lot to offer you from one of its many active volcanoes to its jungle tours of the Mayan temples.
  Add a little color to your trip and visit the city of Flores, which is famous for its warm colored buildings, cobble-stoned streets, and

intimately small beaches.
Take a dip in Lake Atitlan, which is Central America's deepest lake.

- *Honduras*
  Honduras is another island for all the swimmers and water lovers out there! Come here to do some adventurous snorkeling or learn how to dive.
  To learn more about the history of the Mayans head to Copan, which was once a hub for the Mayan government, art, culture, science, and astronomy. Now, you can see these ancient Mayan ruins for yourself! On the site, there are two large pyramids and many stone temples with hieroglyphics depicting Mayan history.

- *Nicaragua*
  Visit Granada, which is one of the country's largest and oldest cities. You'll be able to experience the city's fascinating history and architecture through its amazing sites and museums.
  For an escape from the busy city, make time for one of the islands off the coast of the country.

- *Panama*
  If you're looking for a city experience, go to Panama City, Panama. There, you can find high rise skyscrapers. You can take trips outside the city to the Panama Canal where you can learn about the history of it.
  If you're planning to make your way into South America, Panama City is a perfect transition

city.

- *Costa Rica*
  Anywhere in Costa Rica, you go will be safe, fun, and full of adventure. This country is the one of the best when it comes to eco-tourism. You can visit one of the luscious rainforests and hear tropical birds and chase after waterfalls.
  For adventure seekers, zip line through the rainforest canopies, stay in a tent or an eco-lodge in the jungle.
  For naturalists take a trip to Monteverde, which is home to the Monteverde Cloud Forest Reserve!

South America

- *Chile*
  Chile is a diverse country with many activities and a little bit of everything. This country stretches nearly 2800 miles or 4500 km long, with the Pacific Ocean bordering it to the west, the Andes to the east, and Peru to the north, and the Antarctic to the south.
  Only here can you visit the deserts for a couple weeks and then go on a trek in the glaciers, and finally relax on a beach to round off your stay.

- *Argentina*
  Argentina is one of the larger countries in South America, which means it pulls in a lot of tourists each year. Due to its location, there are

many landscapes to explore based on your interests.

You can discover the glaciers at Glacier National Park and the deserts at Talampaya National Park. The most beautiful attraction is the Iguazu Waterfalls, which is well worth the visit even if it's crowded.

If you're a water person, come to see Iguazu Falls which is a force of nature.

Not much of a nature person?

Visit the urban capital, Bueno Aires, which houses high-end restaurants, fascinating museums, and modern and colonial architecture.

- *Peru*
  Peru is one for the ancient historians and those aspiring to learn more! The country is full of ancient historical gems and archeological sites. Cusco is home to the Inca ruins and proof of the Spanish conquest of the country. Of course, you must go see Machu Picchu in the Andes! The one place that the Spanish could not find and is still well-preserved.

  Lima is a modern beach city where you can learn to surf and relax on the shores.

- *Paraguay*
  Paraguay is one of those underrated countries that is completely safe for female solo travelers. The country offers scenic one-of-a-kind landscapes, waterfalls, natural lakes, and other bodies of water.

  The country is also home to shy and hard to see wildlife such as pumas, jaguars, and tapir. If

you visit Parque Nacional Defensores del Chaco, you just might catch a rare siting of one of these!

- *Uruguay*
Uruguay is a place to escape your stressful life and enter your traveler life.
The country promotes a forward moving and cosmopolitan atmosphere, where many Brazilian and Argentinians vacation. You'll be glad this place isn't overrun with tourists just yet.
There are many beaches where you can relax alone and really think about what you want or invite a few friends to come with you.
Accommodations vary from luxury resorts to small and intimate village homestays to seaside houses.
You can leave the coastline and head for the countryside to relax and sample wines you can only get in Uruguay.

Africa

- *Botswana*
Botswana is a safe and relatively wealthy country compared to others in Africa. The country has a stable economic and political system, which ensures basic rights for everyone.
Overall, Botswana ranks as one of the top countries to visit since its lodges are not fenced in and are up-to-date with eco-sensitive

standards.

The country boasts terrains ranging from deserts to deltas in the inland.

If you're an animal lover, the country has one of the most reliable safari animal sightings.

- *Namibia*
  Namibia is Botswana's neighbor and another safe country thanks to its stable government. This country is an ideal place for desert lovers! It offers a variety of animals, fascinating cultures to learn about, and scenic landscapes. Go to Damaraland to look for elephants in the desert and immerse yourself in the culture with a visit to a Himba village.
  You can try to catch a glimpse of a Black Rhino at the Okaukuejo Waterhole!

- *Ghana*
  Ghana is great since you can travel there at any point during the year! You can enjoy one of the many coastal beaches and experience the local's helpfulness and friendliness.
  Expect to be blown away with the culture in Ghana. Only here, you'll experience culture full of happiness and family and tribal values. Most festivals celebrate the wonderfulness of life and Ghanaians show their love for it through their clothes and artifacts.
  Since this is a coastal country, you can explore forests and chill on beaches.

- *Morocco*
  While other north African countries have become more unstable, Morocco has remained

steady in its economy and government. Chefchaouen, the "Blue City" is one of the most fascinating and beautiful towns in the world. The town is covered in bright blue-cerulean buildings tucked in the hills of the region. The town is very walkable since cars are not allowed on the narrow streets.

- *Ethiopia*
  Ethiopia is a hidden gem in Africa with its diverse and alluring scenery and some of Africa's less famous wildlife.
  The country also has a rich history with sites ranging from 17th century castles to ancient tombs.
  You can visit sprawling cities or arid plains or valleys and mountains.

- *Uganda*
  Uganda is another hidden treasure in Africa. Since it has a rocky history, the tourism industry is still growing. This means, compared to other African countries, it's easier to connect to the local people.
  Uganda is home to Bwindi National park, where you can try to get a peek at the diverse and populated wildlife. You might be able to sight gorillas, African Golden Cats, and a few other animals.

- *Tanzania*
  Tanzania is a great east African option to start your solo travels. There are many coastal towns that have resorts, hostels, and other sites for tourists.

Go see the wildlife and spend some time inland at Ruaha National Park, which has every African animal except for the rhino.

- *Kenya*
  Kenya's improved security and government stability has made it a safe place for solo travelers.
  Best to go to Lake Nakuru National Park, where you can spot up to 2 million flamingos standing at the shore. There, you'll also be able to see other water animals such as hippos in addition to giraffes, impalas, and zebras.
  You can also visit a less visited park such as Meru National Park where you can also catch a glimpse of giraffes and hippos but also lions, elephants, snakes, and numerous bird species.

- *Rwanda*
  Rwanda is rated the safest country in the entire continent and houses the largest tropical forest. You can easily spend your entire time in Rwanda exploring the rainforest and looking for mountain gorillas.
  The hills and mountains in the tropical rainforest have a morning mist, which creates a magical and enchanting scene to wake up to every day.

- *Madagascar*
  Madagascar is famous for its wildlife and the American movie helped promote it.
  If you've seen the movie, you know it promoted lemurs and they're much better seen in the wild. You have the chance to see them when

you plan your visit to this island off of Africa. Once you're done looking for lemurs, you can hop the Manakara Express, a French-era railway that goes up and down the coast. On the ride, you can see one of the most biodiverse places not only on the continent but also the world.

Oceania

- *Australia*
  Australia is easily one of the top-ranked places to travel solo as a female. It is safe and the public transportation is easy to manage in the cities.
  Just as in other counties, I suggest starting your travels in a major city such as Melbourne or Sydney. From either of those cities, you can take day trips or find people to road trip around the country with.
  Research what the wonderful country offers and figure out where you want to go from one of the major cities!
  The Great Barrier Reef is off the coast of Queensland for the most incredible diving in the world. Atherton Tablelands is home to the best waterfalls in the country to satisfy your water craze. Or, if you want to experience the nature without physically moving, take the railway through the scenic backdrop of Daintree National Park.

- *New Zealand*
  New Zealand is a country if you're an outdoor or adventure seeker in this part of the world. This country leads the region in eco-tourism. Auckland's scenic backdrop is made of volcanic craters and a lovely harbor to wander through. Take a hike up to Mount Eden for panoramic views of Auckland or take a dive at Goat Island. Rafting through glowworm caves is just the start of the many unique activities you can do and experience in New Zealand.
  Wherever you end up, you won't be disappointed or bored!

Antarctica

For those of you who like the cold and outdoor adventure, visit Antarctica!

Here, you'll be able to hike, kayak, and do other outdoor exploring activities in the world's most pristine continent. This place is nearly untouched by humans and civilization making a unique and memorable experience.

In order to get to, from, and around Antarctica, you'll take a boat or ship. It's uncommon that commercial planes fly there so you'll need to book a boat from South America.

This place is remote so you'll be able to really bond with the people who come with you. Generally, you'll meet your shipmates, scientists, and other long-term travelers. It will be refreshing to make deep connections with people through a shared experience.

In addition to seeing icebergs, you'll be able to visit penguins up close. These cute animals don't have any fears of humans and are quite curious.

Chapter 3: Bumps on the Road

I've talked a lot about the wonderful things about traveling solo, but haven't touched on the bumps on the road you might face.

Don't let these bumps deter you from traveling solo because they are normal and can easily be overcome!

It might be harder to do while you're traveling solo, but push yourself hard and you'll get through it.

Homesickness

Homesickness is a common bump on the road you might experience.

This just happens when you miss home after a while or are tired of traveling from place to place.

No need to worry about this!

There are a few tips and tricks to "get over" homesickness whenever it creeps on you.

For me, it happened a lot at the beginning of the trip or if I was alone too often and was on my phone.

Here are a few pieces of advice to help you:

- *Put Yourself Out There and Meet New People*
  Don't be alone! Seems like an obvious solution,

right?

Making a few new friends can be a speedy solution for your round of homesickness.

If you're staying in a hostel, get yourself out of the room and into the kitchen or common area. Bring a book or journal instead of your phone. You'll be able to meet someone quickly that way! Ask people simple questions like where are they from, where have they traveled, and the like.

You'll find that travelers want to meet to new people like you! It just takes one person to start the conversation.

Who knows, you might explore the town with these new people or travel together for a little bit.

If the hostel organizes events such as walking tours, family dinners, bar crawls, or similar activities ask to join! It's an easy way to meet people!

If you're in a remote area, ask what activities there are to do. If remote areas aren't working for you, just leave.

- *Go Out on the Town*
  Why did you decide to travel?

  It was probably to see and experience a new culture and food. Go to famous sites such as the Eifel Tower or the temples of Chiang Mai.

  Use these reasons to get out of bed and do the things you want to do! Ask the hostel the best way to get there or just wander around the city! Take a map if you need it.

  Just getting out will help and there's nothing wrong with taking a journal or a book and reading it alone at a café! You might meet a

local there who can give you advice on what to do and where to go.

- *Slow It Down*
  Traveling is very exciting and you might be bouncing to do everything and go everywhere at once!
  Slow. It. Down.
  You'll burn yourself out if you try to fit everything in a day! If your trip is open-ended, take more time in cities you enjoy before going off to the next. You'll be able to make friends more easily and even befriend a local.
  When you take time to breathe and slow down, you'll be able to fully take in your surroundings. Make time to reflect on your days-even if it's just a few words to remind you of it!

- *Write It Out*
  If you have a journal, grab it and your pen! If you don't have one, ask for a piece of paper or five! And then begin writing!
  Get out the negative thoughts in your system and then read it back. You might figure out that some of the negative things aren't as big as you thought!
  Take time to reflect on your travels so far and highlight the positive things that have been happening.
  If you've been keeping a journal regularly, read back on past journal entries. You might be able to see the progress or read about something you may have forgotten about.

- *Treat Yourself*
  Maybe all this traveling is making you tired and tense.
  Splurge on yourself, if you're that type of person. I am not so don't be discouraged if this tip doesn't work for you.
  Take yourself to the spa, eat a nice dessert, or buy yourself something nice.
  If you can't or not willing to shell out the money to indulge, which might contribute to your stress, then don't do it. Find something else to "pamper" yourself with.

- *Challenge Yourself and Learn Something New*
  Did you ever want to learn how to cook or to dance?
  Ask if there is a class you can sign up for. The hostels might organize some themselves!
  This is an easy way to get your mind off of being homesick!
  You'll be able to throw your energy into a new skill and meet new people along the way!

- *Say "Yes"*
  You're the only person stopping yourself from doing something new and exciting!
  If someone from your dorm invites you to dinner, say "yes"!
  If you want to do something, ask someone from the hostel if they'd like to come with you! Or, if someone is going the same way you are, ask if you can join!
  Don't let couples and groups of people intimidate you, they want to meet new people

too.

- *Call Home*
  Call home if you really need to or call a friend you've been keeping on touch with.
  They might be able to empathize with you and help restore your travel motivation.
  Try not to get too involved with things back home, which would help perpetuate your homesickness.

- *Get Off Your Phone*
  Easy, put your phone on airplane mode while you're out exploring! Only take pictures so you won't always be checking your social media platforms.
  Seeing photos from back home will make you wish you were there. When, in fact, you'd rather be where you are currently-not home!

- *Sample from Home*
  While you're traveling, you might not realize how much you like a particular food or drink. This might happen after not eating your favorite home food after an extended period of time.
  You might be able to find it at a specialty store or a very comparable equivalent at a local restaurant.

Culture Shock

Some places you go to might be so different that you feel a little unsettled.

Don't worry, like homesickness, it is easy to overcome and a common bump to experience.

Remember, if you're feeling too unsettled to the point of being uncomfortable, then you might need to leave.

But, before you think of leaving, try these tips:

- *Do Your Research*
  Before you go, brush up on the cultural differences you should expect. For example, if you're traveling through the Middle East, read about what is acceptable for women to wear. Be aware that women may still be thought of as the weaker sex. This is especially important if you're from western countries. You might not have all the same rights as you do back home.

- *Learn Where and Where Not to Go*
  The last place you want to end up is in a rough part of town. You'll stick out, which will make you feel uncomfortable and puts you in a compromising situation.
  Use a travel guide to learn where to go and where not to go. This will guarantee you won't book a hostel on the "wrong side of the train tracks" so to say.
  This doesn't mean that you have to stick to the touristy areas all the time!
  Just be careful.

Ask your hostel or hotel what are the safe, calmer places in a city to visit.

- *Learn the Language*
Learn what language is spoken in whatever country you're going to! You don't need to be fluent, by any means, before you arrive. However, knowing a few phrases goes a long way! Locals will appreciate the effort when you ask them for help.

- *Hygiene*
Research the hygiene standards in different countries. This is especially true in some Asian countries. Most of them have squat toilets instead of western ones. And, showers might just be a bucket and water.
Be sure that you're ready to handle all the changes! And, remember, it's all part of the experience! You'll get used to it or go home.
On the flip side, some countries might have higher hygiene standards than your home country! For example, it might be customary to take a shower before you leave the house every time.

- *Embrace the Differences*
Remember, you wanted to travel to experience new cultures!
Embrace the differences between the country your visiting and your home country.
A change of attitude can make the biggest difference. Instead of saying I don't like how crowded this city is, say wow there are so many

people here I can meet.

- *Check the Calendar*
Check the calendar of the country you're going to visit. There might be a local festival or holiday going on!
Read up on it so you can understand why people celebrate it and be able to appreciate the holiday more.
On the other side, a holiday could mean that the city will be emptier or there won't be as many shops open. This is especially true in Europe during the later summer months.

- *Be Patient*
Getting over culture shock won't happen in a day. Give it a few days or more so you can adjust and finally feel more at ease.
If you're really feeling discouraged, take some time for yourself. Find a quiet place in the city to regroup.

- *Remind Yourself Why You Traveled*
When traveling becomes really rough, remind yourself why you started in the first place.
Keep your reasons for traveling in mind, write them down, and read them aloud to yourself.

Sexual Harassment

Sexual harassment is just a reality you have to deal with as a female solo traveler. And, just being a woman in general.

As unfortunate as it is, sexual harassment doesn't disappear while you're traveling and you can't let your guard down.

You could be lucky and not have to deal with it while you're traveling or experience the "low end" of it.

I've heard about women who have been sexually harassed at different levels in every city they visit.

And, I've also heard about and met women who haven't even been catcalled or followed around.

Even though sexual harassment is prevalent throughout the world, it is more common in some cities than others.

Don't let this scare you or change your mind about traveling!

It's important to be aware of and how to handle.

Here are a few tips about how to deal with sexual harassment while traveling:

- *Follow the "Dress Code"*
  Research what country or countries you're traveling to and try to dress like the locals. You won't draw that much attention to yourself if you blend in. Dressing like a tourist and acting too much like one will make you stand out.
  Some locals like to just pick on the tourists or think that girls on vacations are just there to "have a fun time" with a local.

You might also experience sexual harassment from male travelers. Some men think that they can have any girl they want. Or, that they're taking a vacation from their partners or spouses.

If this happens, especially in a hostel or guided tours, immediately tell the manager or tour guide.

- *Research Cultural Norms*
  Along with doing research on the "dress code" of different countries, also educate yourself about cultural norms.

  Keep in mind, an action that may be inappropriate to you is actually a sign of admiration to them.

  For example, men in Costa Rica often make sounds at women from their cars. This actually is a compliment not a type of catcall.

  This type of behavior, may not be tolerated if you're from Europe or North America. But, you have to brush it off.

  Keep in mind, in a scenario like Costa Rica, those men didn't know they offended you. They really wanted to give you a compliment.

  If you're not sure how to feel about a situation, ask a local or someone at the hostel.

- *Be Loud and Don't Give Up*
  If something happens to you, no matter where you are, draw attention to yourself.

  Make a scene, get noticed, and people will help you. Someone might even speak up for you if the harasser is claiming ignorance.

One of my friends was groped on a metro. She yelled "What are you doing? I didn't ask you to rub yourself on me!"

Immediately, a few people turned their heads and caught him in the act. At the next stop, they all got off with her and went to the metro police. They took the man away from her, took her statement, and wrote witness reports. Everything else was taken care of from there. This incident happened in Europe, so don't expect every police system to be the same as the westernized countries.

- *Contact the Police*

  In my friend's case, the police took care of everything and were very supportive. They were on her side and actually wanted to help. Remember, this won't be the case everywhere you travel to. In some cases, the police might give you a hard time for even asking to report the incident.

  In a more patriarchal society, police might just write a report and do nothing else. Or worse, demand a bribe since you're a foreigner.

  Having said that, it's still best to know the local emergency number. For more serious scenarios such as rape or assault, it's best to contact your embassy first and go from there.

- *Use Your "Travel Smarts"*

  There's no need to travel in fear!
  Use your "travel smarts" which is the same strategies you use back home.

For example, walk on well-lit streets at night, don't have your phone out when you're on the streets, and try to travel with a buddy at night. Trust your instincts, if something doesn't feel right, or if someone is making you feel uncomfortable. Just get out of there. Don't wait for the situation to escalate and have an exit strategy.
You truly don't need a self-defense class or have pepper spray with you. Use common sense and trust your gut when it comes to potentially compromising situations.

- *Have the Right Attitude*
  When you know you're likely to experience sexual harassment, such as at a nightclub or walking down the street, make sure you have the right attitude and plan.
  If you speak out, don't be surprised if you don't change the country's culture immediately. Ponder if it's even your place to have the main role in this culture change.
  If the local police take your claim seriously, don't be afraid to follow all the way through.

Hostel Roommates

It's the truth.

You won't like every person you meet in the hostel, especially in your dorm room.

Perhaps, one of your hostel roommates snores loudly. Or, another roommate "stores" his or her things everywhere.

Whatever the problem, may be, there is a solution!

In this section, I'll go over common hostel roommate problems and how to resolve respectfully and cope with it.

- *Food Disappears*
  Some hostels have a shared kitchen or pantry for their guests. When there are a lot of guests in the hostel, it's a common mistake to take someone else's food.
  If this happens to you, try not to take it personally.
  To remedy this, label all your food and ask if something doesn't have a label. Most hostels have a label system in place so it might not even happen to you.

- *Noisy Hostel Roommates*
  If you've ever lived in university dorms, you can relate to noisy roommates.
  It can be anything from accidentally turning on the lights at night to making too much noise in the morning.
  Remember, noisy roommates may not be disturbing you on purpose, but nevertheless it's still annoying.
  If your bed doesn't come with a curtain, try sleeping with either a sleeping mask, earplugs, or both.
  You might get lucky and not have to deal with

noisy roommates.

- *Messy Roommates*
  Another roommate you might have experienced in university is the messy roommate.
  Keep in mind being messy is relative so don't be really harsh when this happens. Some people like to pack a lot and don't realize there's not a place to store it in the hostel.
  Just ask someone if they could not spread their things around the room. If they still don't get it, explain that you also need the space as well.

- *The Roommate Who Makes You Feel Uncomfortable*
  If someone in your hostel dorm room makes you feel uncomfortable, either sexually or nonsexual, ask them to stop.
  Immediately, collect any "evidence" that made you feel uncomfortable and tell a manager. They are trained to handle these types of situations and can switch rooms for you. In some cases, they might even kick the other person out if his or her behavior was inappropriate.

- *Dirty Shower*
  Not all roommates remember to clean out the shower when they're done. Sometimes they might leave a pile of hair or have flooded the bathroom.
  It's hard to pinpoint which hostel roommate did it and it may not be from your room. In fact, it could be a collective effort.

To get around this, just bring your own toiletries and your sandals into the shower.

- *"Fast Friends"*
  Of course, one of the reasons to stay in hostels is to meet new people! That is great and encouraged, especially as a solo traveler.
  Don't let every friendly person make you put your guard down. Remember, these people are strangers and could steal your things.
  Unfortunately, there isn't a "silent code" where everyone looks out for each other's valuables. Just use the lock on your locker and keep your valuables (phone, charger, wallet, passport, etc.) in there at all times.
  Bottom line: Keep your wits with you and you'll be able to make friends and not lose your valuables.

- *Bittersweet Farewells*
  Unfortunately, when you're traveling you'll have to depart from anyone you meet along the way. Even if you guys travel together, it too comes to an end.
  It's just the sad reality of constantly being on the go.
  Remember, while the farewells are bittersweet, we do live with modern technology! Figure out how you want to stay in touch, whether that be Instagram, WhatsApp, or Facebook.
  You may not message each other every day, but you'll be so glad when you do get that occasional message. You'll also have a personal guide if you end up visiting their home country.

Traveler's Sick

At some point on your travels, you'll get sick. It's unavoidable and it happens when you're on the go so often.

Germs are on buses, trains, hostels, airplanes, and other places.

Don't worry if it's just a common cold. Just take it easy for a few days and you'll be fine.

If it's something worse, you might have to seek more advanced medical care.

In that case, ask a hostel staff member, or host if you're staying elsewhere, what's the best place to go.

In western Europe, parts of the Middle East and Asia, the medical systems and treatment is current with contemporary practices and instruments.

If you're going to a developing country, you might want to look up what your medical options are before arriving. Just to be prepared for the worst-case scenario.

Best tip: Wash your hands and wash them often, get plenty of rest, and check if you can drink the tap water!

Chapter 4: Where to Stay

While you're traveling, you can stay in different types of accommodations such as hostels, hotels, an Airbnb, and homestays.

It depends on your comfort level, budget, and what type of traveler you are.

Remember, you don't have to exclusively stay in one type of accommodation or another.

For example, maybe you need some privacy after staying in hostels for a month, so you decide to book a hotel room for a night.

Or, you want a more home-style immersive experience so you try a homestay.

Whatever you choose, remember to read the reviews before booking it! You don't want to show up to a place that doesn't suit you.

In this chapter, I'll briefly discuss your different lodging options.

Hotels

Hotels provide short-term lodging for travelers. The quality of the hotels can range from a humble room with a bed and bathroom to a large suite with high-quality beds and possible kitchen supplies.

A hotel room typically houses one to six or more people in a room or suite.

It can be nice if you're traveling with a few friends and want to have some more privacy for a few nights. It might even be comparable to a nicer hostel in terms of price tag.

If you're a traveler that highly values having your own space, security, and privacy, then hotels may be the way to go!

Or, maybe you normally travel by hostel, but need a night to yourself, then splurging on a hotel room is not a bad idea. Believe me, after staying in hostels, having one night to yourself will be a blessing.

Remember, while having your own space is nice, hotels aren't as social as hostels. The hotel might have a bar to meet other guests, but they normally don't organize events such as family dinners or bar crawls. They might have some common space in the lobby but typically don't.

Hostels

Simply put, a hostel is a budget-friendly accommodation with at least one dormitory room and a common area. Some nicer hostels have a "free" breakfast you can take advantage of. Others might even have kitchens to help you and your budget.

If you're a solo traveler, on a budget, or enjoy meeting other people, then hostels are the choice for you!

Hostels make it easy to meet other travelers and like-minded people. The hostels organize group walking tours around the city and happy hours. This makes it easy to meet people from all over the world.

Typically, when you decide to stay at a hostel, you book a night instead of a room. You could stay in a room with just four other people or up to twenty. Depends on your comfort level and budget.

Hostels are secure places, despite what you may have heard. They have lockers and provide locks if you don't have one. They also have secure luggage and storage rooms if you're taking a day trip.

The downside to staying in a hostel is the same as staying in a university dorm. You can expect to have little privacy, one bathroom per floor or section, and risk of theft. These are just a common few cons to hostels.

However, if you can look past the few disadvantages of staying in a hostel, then you can have a wonderful experience there.

While I stayed in hostels, I met some really great people and explored the city I was visiting. I still keep in touch with a few of these friends to this day. I never had a problem with security or having my valuables stolen. If there weren't proper lockers in my dorm, I carried my valuables on me.

Airbnb

Airbnb is an online platform that connects homeowners or apartment dwellers with people who are looking for accommodation. Hosts list their places and "rent" out their houses to travelers. Your accommodation could be a room in a house, a suite of rooms, an apartment, a boat, or an entire house.

If you're looking for something more personable than a hotel with the independence of a hostel, then an Airbnb could work for you.

It's best to split an Airbnb with friends so the cost would be comparable or even cheaper than a nice hotel room. This is especially helpful if you just want a "friend's weekend" and want more privacy, security, and space than what a hostel can offer.

Booking an Airbnb is great since you can stay in a local's place and possibly be shown around by your host. In addition, you might end up in a quieter neighborhood away from the main touristy areas.

The downside, like hotels, it's hard to meet new people if you're staying in a residential or quiet part of town.

Homestays

Homestays allow you to stay in the home of a local for a night or up to a year. You can get out of the big cities and really experience what it's like to live in the country. Sometimes, you can arrange a stay where you do work around the house in exchange for lodging and sometimes food.

If you're looking for a quiet town or village, then try to arrange a homestay with a family. This option is much safer than Couchsurfing since you know what is expected of you. You might even pick up a few handy skills through your host family.

Before you stay, you'll agree with your host what type of accommodation will be provided and what type of work, if any, you'd be doing. Not all homestays want you to do work.

If you want to improve your foreign language skills this is a great way to practice. You can possibly become fluent if you've had some training prior to the homestay.

Homestays do come with some cons just like hostels and hotels. For example, accommodation could be very basic or your host has rules you must adhere to.

Worst case, you and your host don't get along and you leave earlier than planned.

I enjoyed my homestay experience and slowly transitioned to farms. I like having more structure in my days and learning new skills.

Bed and Breakfast

Bed and Breakfasts are similar to homestays. You get to stay in lodging overnight or for a few and are fed breakfast in the morning. Often these establishments are family-run with a few other staff members.

Unlike homestays, the lodging is more than basic and you can expect to have a private room and bathroom. You'll have some rules, but not as many as some homestays. You'll also have more freedom to explore the city. Bed and Breakfasts usually aren't too far from the nearest big town.

Bed and breakfast accommodation is a nice middle ground between homestays and hostels. You get the independence and social aspect of hostels with the home comforts of a homestay.

Chapter 5: Volunteering

Volunteering is a great way to immerse yourself in a different culture and lifestyle while giving back to the community.

I highly suggest doing this at least once while you're traveling. If you don't like it, by all means, don't travel in that style.

You're not limited to just farming! As I mentioned in the previous section, some homestays will let you work in exchange for accommodation and food.

In this chapter, I'll briefly list the different ways to volunteer and websites to help make it a reality!

Available Opportunities

When you think of volunteering while traveling, farming might be the first thought. I know that not everyone wants to farm or be in remote areas.

I've put together a small list to help you find a volunteer opportunity suitable to you.

- *Environmental Conservation*
  Are you eco-friendly and concerned about your ecological footprint?
  An environmental conservation volunteer trip would fit you perfectly!
  With a volunteer position like this, you can

explore, understand, and work with different ecosystems in various countries!
You can go to really interesting places such as Fiji to work in the forest or Antarctica to study the changing climate and melting glaciers.

- *"It Takes a Village to Raise a Child"*
  Do you remember the Igbo and Yoruba proverb "It takes a village to raise a child"?
  You have that ability at home and abroad! There are opportunities for you to help build villages in rural and urban areas around the world. Even if the village is nearly done, you can help put the finishing touches on it. You'll also be able to meet and help families who will be living in the houses you build.
  For example, there are programs in Brazil and Nicaragua, where you help build basic brick houses that have bathrooms and kitchens.

- *Teach English*
  Teaching English is a popular volunteering activity among travelers. You can also get paid for it!
  If you're not sure if you like teaching, this is a low-stress opportunity to try it.
  There are so many organizations that arrange trips where you teach English. Since knowledge of the English language is so valuable, you can go to South America, Europe, and Asia!
  Some programs don't require any prior experience and will train you!

- *Cultural and Historical Immersion*
  One of the reasons you travel is to learn about a

country's historical and cultural background! There are ways for you to deeply learn about a country's history and culture. This can be done through conservation work. You can learn about how old artwork is kept safe and restored.

- *Take Care of a Trail*
  You can combine your love for hiking and nature preservation in a volunteer position. This is especially popular for traveling around the United States on a budget.
  You'll be able to work either in a national park or trail, where you'll be doing trail maintenance, signage and possibly building new trail structures.

- *Take Care of Animals*
  Besides teaching English, taking care and working with animals is the second most popular volunteer opportunity.
  You can choose to work directly with the animals such as helping feed them or documenting behavior for traits.
  If you're more of a hands-off person, there are opportunities for you to learn more about endangered animals and conservation efforts.

- *Farming*
  Farming is a great way to give back to a community and live in a smaller town or village for a few weeks!
  You'll walk away with, hopefully, a few new friends, and new skills to share!
  Farms can vary in size and work so be sure you

and your host are clear about expectations. Worst case, you leave earlier than planned. Some work is very labor intensive and this depends on the farm so double-check what you're getting yourself into.
Generally, you'll work 4-5 hours a day and then have the rest of the day to explore. You'll share or help prepare at least one meal with your host too!

- *Hostels*
  Some hostels, need volunteers to work for them, especially during the high season. You can work in exchange for a bed in the hostel. You'll be responsible for your food, but it does help your budget!
  In a hostel, you might work at the front desk, help clean, lead city tours, or even bar crawls. For hostels, you don't even have to apply online, sometimes being there and getting along with the staff will get you a position.

Websites

Now, that you know what's available, you can choose which volunteer opportunity you like!

Next question: How can I make these volunteer ideas a reality?

There are websites that connect volunteers such as you to hosts or organizations that create volunteer trips.

To make it easier for you, I've researched different sites for you to choose from. The list isn't extensive, but it will give you a good start!

- GoEco
  This website helps connect volunteer and hosts for a variety of volunteer opportunities.
  This is a good website to start with if you're interested in environmental and conservation work. You can also find opportunities to work with animals and other wildlife.
  Trips can range from ecological work in a dense jungle to taking care of animals on a safari. The websites organize the trip for you so all you need to do is show up!

- GoVolunteering
  GoVolunteering organizes trips for volunteers who want to build structures. Or, if you want to learn a few construction and carpentry skills. You can sign up for a trip that helps build simple houses for villages.
  You can also find trips that focus on art conservation and restoration through GoVolunteering!
  There's a variety on the site so search and find your match!

- Power to the People
  Power to the People is partnered with GoVolunteering and geared towards work in Nicaragua.
  There you can combine green construction and community building. You'll most likely be in a

small village and help build or maintain it.

- WorldTeach
World Teach is one of many websites that connects English teachers with villages and language centers that need them!
You don't need any prior experience with some organizations! They can train you on how to teach English.
You could be teaching kids, teens, or even adults.

- American Hiking Society
American Hiking Society is for those traveling through the United States.
You can work anywhere within the country from California's Redwood to Acadia National Park in Maine.
What more?
You can find your volunteer opportunity based on accommodation, state, and work level! You just have to use the filters on the website's search engine.

- WWOOF
WWOF stands for World Wide Organization of Organic Farmers.
On this site, you can search by country for farms that need volunteers and what months they accept them.
You can see pictures of the farm and sometimes your accommodation and former volunteers.
Be sure to read the reviews and "interview" through the messaging portal or Skype before

arranging your stay.

- Workaway
  Workaway is similar to WWOOF, but it offers more than just farms!
  While you can find wonderful farms to volunteer on, you can also find homestays, Aupair, hostels, communities, and so much more!
  If you're really not sure what type of volunteering you like, Workaway would be a good option. You can try a handful of different types without signing up for multiple memberships.

Chapter 6: Finding Work

While you're traveling from place to place, you may get tired or run low on money.

Or, perhaps your plan, all along, was to find a place you like and settle there for a few years.

Understandably, you're tired of coming home and saving up for your next adventure. You'd rather just find work as you travel.

There are so many people out there like you, who want endless travels, and to work not in their home country.

You don't need a degree in international studies or business to work overseas. Believe me, there are other ways! Think a little, talk to different people, and get creative!

There are a million ways to make money as you travel ranging from teaching to working in a hostel or backpacker bar.

In this section, I'll discuss the different opportunities, how to find work and specific examples of the most common ones.

Available Opportunities

There are so many options for you when it comes to finding work while traveling.

Sometimes, it happens when you're not trying.

Are you not sure where to start?

Don't worry, it can be a little overwhelming to figure it out.

Here's a list to help start your brainstorming!

- Teaching English
- Peace Corps
- Ski Instructor
- Freelancing
- Au Pair
- Nonprofit work in developing countries
- Research Trips
- University internships
- Dive Master
- Working Holiday Visa

Maybe none of the jobs listed above interest you.

And, that's ok!

You can rule it out and figure out ways to find something you like. A simple internet search can do wonders.

How to Find Work

Finding work can be stressful depending on your circumstances.

How fast you find work depends on what type of job you want and where you are.

For example, some Asian countries need more English teachers than others. I'd talk to people and do your research before picking a country.

I highly recommend waiting until you find somewhere you like before looking for a job. Doing so gives you a chance to "feel out" the place and make sure it's a good fit. You can check out the neighborhood and what accommodations might be available to you.

Going to a place you'd like to work and introducing yourself works best, especially after exploring a town for a week or two.

And, who knows, other opportunities might open themselves up!

Don't give up hope if your first choice doesn't work. You'll find something more suitable for you.

If you're looking for more "professional" work, then I'd research companies in a country you like and apply that way.

Working Holiday Visas

A working holiday visa allows travelers, such as you, to seek gainful employment in a country that provides these types of visas.

With this type of visa, you can live in a different country, work, and save a little bit of money. You can use your savings to travel to neighboring countries after the visa expires!

This visa is popular with younger travelers since it enables them to live in a foreign country and earn money. This visa saves you the time and expense of obtaining a work sponsorship. It's also cheaper than a university study abroad program.

The majority of these visas are offered under a corresponding agreement between a select number of countries. The point is to promote and encourage cultural exchange between different nationalities.

Working holiday visas do come with a few restrictions:

- There is an age limit since it is intended for young travelers. Usually, the age restriction is 18-30 or 35 depending on the country.
- Employment type and length of time in the country is limited.
- Travelers must have enough savings to live off of while looking for employment.
- Travelers must have some type of traveler's or health insurance for the entire stay unless the country covers them.

While I was traveling around South-East Asia, I met a handful of friends who obtained a working holiday visa. They either worked in Australia or New Zealand. After their visa expired, they traveled around Asia before going elsewhere.

After talking to my friends, here are a few tips they passed long:

- Save up more than you need for the plane ticket and living expenses in your desired country.
- Obtain the visa.
- Fly over and then find a job.
- Use social media platforms such as Facebook to find jobs or housing.

If you're curious about what is out there, here is a list of countries that offer the visa:

- Andorra
- Argentina
- Australia
- Austria
- Belgium
- Brazil
- Canada
- Chile
- China
- Colombia
- Costa Rica
- Croatia
- Cyprus
- Czech Republic
- Denmark
- Estonia
- Finland
- France
- Germany
- Greece

- Hong Kong
- Hungary
- Iceland
- Indonesia
- Ireland
- Israel
- Italy
- Japan
- Latvia
- Lithuania
- Luxembourg
- Malaysia
- Malta
- Mexico
- Monaco
- Netherlands
- New Zealand
- Norway
- Peru
- Philippines
- Poland
- Portugal
- Romania
- Russia
- Singapore
- Slovakia
- Slovenia
- South Africa
- South Korea
- Spain
- Sweden
- Switzerland
- Taiwan

- Thailand
- Turkey
- Ukraine
- United Kingdom
- Uruguay
- Vietnam

A lot of countries offer this special type of visa. Unfortunately, not every country opens its doors to everyone. You'll have to research which countries allow you to apply for a working holiday visa.

Teaching English and Certifications

Teaching English is one of the most popular jobs expats pick up! Unlike working holiday visas, you're not limited by your nationality for this position!

This topic is also very complex and deep and can be its own guide! For purposes of this book, I'll give you a general overview of it and what certifications you can earn.

Most jobs require that you have a strong grasp of the English language and some don't even require any prior experience.

Unfortunately, this job does play favorites to those who have white skin and come from native English-speaking countries. This trend is more prevalent in South East Asia than anywhere else in the world.

For example, I could have a Teaching English as a Foreign Language (TEFL) certificate, university degree, and a United Kingdom passport. But if I have Asian heritage, I'd have a harder time getting a job.

This doesn't mean it's impossible for people of color to find teaching jobs. It just makes it harder. More persistence is needed and you'll find a job.

Visas and Work Permits

Visas are a little tricky for this topic since it depends on what country you decide to teach in. Generally, it's better to arrive and apply for a tourist visa that gives you time to find a job.

After finding a job, you can apply for a business or renew your tourist visa. Some countries also require a work permit in *addition* to your visa.

Unfortunately, holding a business visa in some countries does not mean you can legally work there. Sounds confusing. Just to be clear, in some countries you need two documents: a business visa and a work permit.

For a work permit, you need an employer or even a friend to be your "sponsor".

The perks of a work permit are the peace of mind it gives you. You won't have to worry about renewing your visa as long as you have your sponsor.

Highly Rated Countries to Work In

As I mentioned before, you can teach English anywhere in the world that needs teachers.

I wanted to list the highly-rated countries for English teachers. You aren't limited to the countries listed in this section! You can at least consider them while you're looking for work.

Remember, no two English teachers are alike. You might like countries in South America while another like those in the Middle East.

- *Cambodia*
  Cambodia, like other South-Eastern Asian countries, is beautiful and full of rich and dark history that's waiting for you to dive into! The landscape changes from rice paddies and fertile plains to waterfalls and crater lakes! Cambodia's job market is exploding and English teachers are in high demand. You can easily find a job any time of the year, especially in Phnom Penh. Compared to other Asian countries, the salary is modest. However, the low cost of living makes it manageable for expats.

- *Mexico*
  Mexico is known for its extensive cultural and natural sites and attractions. After visiting one, you'll be awestruck and possibly inspired. You can wander through Mexico City or visit the

Mayan ruins in Tulum.

Just like Cambodia, you can find work year-round, lest major holidays such as Christmas and Easter.

You'll have the most luck of finding a job in one of the bigger cities. Try Mexico City, Guadalajara, Puebla, Juarez, Puerto Vallarta, and Leon.

- *Vietnam*

  Vietnam is another country whose job market is vastly expanding and in high need of English teachers.

  This country is diverse: you have the rice fields in Sapa and popping street markets in Ho Chi Minh City (Saigon). Of course, you also have the Mekong River to cruise on your holidays from teaching.

  Many of Vietnam's highly rated English teaching centers prefer native speakers with at least a bachelor's degree. Smaller schools may not be as picky, but be aware those requirements exist.

- *Nicaragua*

  Nicaragua offers welcoming beaches, wonderful landscapes, and a high need for English teachers.

  Unlike other Central American countries, this one is still "undiscovered" and not many tourists come through each year. This will let you have a more intimate and unique experience. It will be as if you're uncovering new things every day!

  Best to start your work search in bigger cities

such as Managua, Grenada, and Leon.

- *Colombia*
  Don't let Colombia's dicey reputation scare you away! This country is full of beaches, rainforests, and rich history and culture!
  The economic and political situation is stable and growing, which means there is a demand for English teachers.
  As other countries, try looking for work in bigger cities, to begin with. After, you might be able to find jobs through your friends and former employers.

- *Czech Republic*
  Do medieval castles, stone streets, and quaint villages, appeal to you?
  Czech Republic might be the place for you! Along with its history, there are plenty of modern-day businesses such as nightclubs and cafes to go to.
  This is a popular destination for American expats since it is easy to get a legal work permit to teach. Additionally, the cost of living is lower here compared to western Europe.
  This country is also a good middle ground between eastern and western Europe.

- *Taiwan*
  Taiwan combines the old with the new! This country boasts a high-tech industry in a tropical landscape. The combination alone makes the experience different than other countries you could teach in.
  Most jobs will be centered in Taipei, the

nation's capital.
While there are beaches on the outer parts, you can find mountains to hike and cycle through! There's also a handful of hot springs for you to relax in.

- *South Korea*
  South Korea is one of the most modern countries in Asia to teach and is home to generations of history and modern and high-tech urban centers.
  An ideal teaching package comes with free airfare, housing, and a salary that will help teachers save at least $1000/month after expenses. This package is offered for the most highly-rated and experienced teachers.
  Don't worry if this isn't you! If you want that, get experience and talk to people who have taught there!

- *Spain*
  Spain is one of the strongest countries in terms of its need for English teachers. Former teachers say the best time to find work is September-October and then again after the holidays in January.
  Try starting your job search in Madrid before going to another city. Smaller towns might be a better bet since they are less known and jobs are not as competitive.

- *China*
  China is one of the most populated countries and growing each year. This means that the job market is steady for English teachers and the

most profitable. The country is expansive and waiting to be explored! This country is prominent for its history and its influence on the rest of the world.

Teaching Online

Maybe, teaching in-person is not your thing or you like the idea of teaching online and making your own schedule.

That option is available to you and you're not alone! There are so many online teachers that make a living that way.

Teaching online gives you the flexibility to teach and live wherever you want.

How do you start teaching online?

You have three options to find work:

1. Apply to online teaching jobs through an established company.
2. Offer your teaching services on freelancing websites.
3. Build your own private "studio" of students.

If you're a new teacher, I suggest working for an established company, to start. This company would help connect you with employers, give you teacher training, and help with any technical issues.

When you're looking for an established company, find one that has hours in your time zone. Otherwise, you'll work at odd times. Also, be sure you create a profile that stands out from the thousands of teachers out there. While the platforms are great, they do attract a large number of teachers.

Once you've narrowed down your search, look for online reviews about those companies. And avoid any companies that ask for a payment from the start. It's normal if they take a cut from your paycheck as a finder's fee.

After you build up your teaching skills, you can look for more opportunities and possibly freelance or build a private "studio". You can find jobs and advice through Facebook groups associated with teaching English.

When you pursue the freelance or private "studio" option, the most important part is marketing. Be specific in what you can offer students, what age range you teach, how you teach, and price. Have a strong cancellation policy in place as well.

Certifications

As I mentioned many times already, you can earn a certificate to teach English as a second language. Now, I'll talk more about it so you can decide if this option is for you or not.

While there are many options out there, the most well-known certifications are:

1. Teaching English as a Foreign Language (TEFL)
2. Teaching English to Speakers of Other Languages (TESOL)
3. English Language Teaching (ELT)
4. English as a Second Language (ESL)
5. Certificate in Teaching English to Speakers of Other Languages (CELTA), formerly Certificate in Teaching English Language to Adults

All of the certificates are fundamentally the same. They all give you the tools to be a better teacher. There just happens to be an expanding market for TEFL and TESOL certified teachers.

The more prestigious language centers around the world might require a 120-hour TEFL or TESOL certification.

A CELTA certification is a little different than the other ones listed. CELTA has a very strict course regime and only Cambridge certified instructors teach the course. This means, that you're paying for a highly-valued course with a guaranteed quality. It makes your resume/CV standout among other English teachers in the application pool.

Having said that, CELTA is not the only highly regarded certification to earn. There are many that offer the same standards or even better. The chief difference is that with a CELTA the course quality is guaranteed. For a TEFL, do your research and be sure the company is reputable and the certification is what you want.

However, most schools just want to see that you have a certification. It doesn't have to be TEFL or TESOL, just any certification from a recognized and reputable company.

A highly recognized and prestigious language center will want a certificate and lots of teaching experience. If this is your goal, then I would figure out a plan on how to achieve it!

Dive Master

Dive Master is a way to earn money and travel! This option is great if you like the water, swimming, and being active. Consider it if you enjoy farming but need a break from the land.

This section will outline how to earn your Dive Master and Dive Instructor Certifications according to Professional Association of Diving Instructors (PADI).

After trying scuba diving, at least once, and deciding to pursue the option, here are your next steps:

1. First, earn Advanced Open Water Dive and Rescue Diver certificates along with at least 40 logged dives. These are prerequisites to the Dive Master Certification.

2. Second, earn your Dive Master certificate, which will teach you how to lead diving activities along with safety and emergency situations.

3. Third, you can earn more certificates and specializations within the Dive Master realm on your way to Dive Instructor.

4. Fourth, on your way to Dive Instructor, you must earn your Open Water, Advanced Open Water Diver, and Rescue Diver Certificates.

There are many companies, where you can earn your Dive Master and Dive Instructor certifications; however, PADI is the most recognized and reputable company.

Remember, you can earn the certification anywhere. After, you can stay in that country or move to a different one to pursue job prospects.

Au Pair

An Au Pair is another job that allows you to stay with a family, immerse yourself in a new culture and lifestyle, and earn money. Your main duties are cooking, cleaning, and taking care of the children.

While this sounds a lot like a live-in nanny, job, what makes this job different is the cultural exchange. Au Pairs are purposely hired from different countries because the parents want their children to have a rich childhood.

In this section, I'll outline how to become an Au Pair and a few common questions everyone asks.

Here's how to get started:

1. *Select a Country*
   Choose a country you'd like to live and work in for a year.
   Ask yourself what are you looking for in a town or country. This will help things run smoothly down the line.
   You wouldn't want to end up in a small town in France if you're a big city person.

2. *Use an Agency, or Not*
   You can use an agency to find a family or do it independently.
   Using an agency comes with benefits such as visa application and help while you're working. However, these agencies charge a very expensive fee, which may not be worth it.
   All the au pairs I met and interviewed for this book, highly recommended using either aurpairworld.com or greataupair.com

3. *Select a Family*
   Selecting a family is a lot like picking a farmstay or homestay host.
   Scroll around on the site and read the family's profile and look at the pictures, if there are any. Make sure to interview with the family on Skype to ensure it will be a good fit.

4. *Apply for Your Visa*
   This step is complicated to explain since it depends on what passport you hold. For example, a lot of European au pairs' wages weren't reported since they hold European Union passports.
   It's not a good idea to work under the table in a foreign country! Just do the right research to obtain your visa. It's better to live legally, have rights, and access to healthcare.

5. *Figure Out Your Finances*
   Make sure your finances are taken care of well before you leave.
   Remember, to apply for a travel credit card and search for a bank that doesn't charge international fees.
   Have at least $3000-4000 in your bank account before leaving. In the worst case, you need to leave your family, you can take care of yourself while looking for work.
   Let your banks know when, where, and how long you'll be traveling.
   And, last, set up a bank account in the country you're living in. You can ask your family which bank is best.

Common Questions

- *How often can you travel as an au pair?*
  This depends on the family and what you've set up with them. Sometimes, you get time off to explore the country or surrounding ones. Other times, the family may take you

on vacation with them.

- *What are the accommodations like?*
  This again depends on the family and what the country requires. Most likely, you'll have a private room in the house. However, make sure you ask this when you're interviewing the family.
  Sometimes, you'll have your own apartment which gives you, even more, privacy, freedom and makes it easier to find friends.

- *How can you make friends?*
  Making friends while you're working is hard anywhere and living with a family makes it more difficult.
  It's possible to make friends through the activities you do every day. For example, a friend of mine met a couple other au pairs while picking up the family's kids from school.
  If you have time, you can try to find groups that share the same interest as you. If you're a runner, look for running groups that meet regularly.

- *How much can an au pair make?*
  The salary of an au pair is more of a stipend or pocket money. It's meant for you to use it to explore the town and immerse yourself in the culture.
  Your actual "salary" is food and accommodation for the year.
  You can negotiate your stipend when you interview the family. Take into account the

cost of living and how much activities cost in that country.

- *Do I need a driver's license?*
  This actually depends on where your family lives and how close things are. Some families might loan you a car to pick up the kids or go grocery shopping.
  If you want a car for either work or personal use, be upfront about it during the interview process. Also, be sure to check what the rules are for a foreigner driving other people's cars.

Freelancing

Freelancing is the dream that allows you can do what you're good at and like to make money.

It's flexible and you can be your own boss.

You can choose to be what you want as a freelancer. You're not limited to what you studied at university.

For example, I did not study English, journalism, or communication at university. When I decided to try freelancing, I felt that writing was my strongest skills and went from there.

Freelancing can be hard to start depending on what you decide to freelance and specialize in.

Freelancing in computer science and programming is much easier to get started in than most fields. This is just because programmers are in high demand.

Don't give up hope if programming is not your skill or interest! There are ways to grow your skill from a side job to a self-sustained business.

Follow these tips and you'll be freelancing in no time!

- *Write Down Your Goals*
  It will be hard to achieve your goals if you don't have any! Write down what you want to get out of freelancing.
  Do you want freelancing as a side job to earn extra money?
  Or, do you want freelancing to turn into a full-time job?
  Or, is the goal something not listed above? Also, ask yourself why you're freelancing and does it help reach your big picture goals.
  Once you have your big picture goals written out, you can create smaller ones and milestones to help reach the big goals.

- *Specialize in a Lucrative Skill*
  Pick a skill you're good at or one you've been honing during your spare time.
  There will be a lot of competitors in whatever field you choose that charge extremely low rates.
  Don't compete on rates because your work should be valued. Sites such as UpWork and Fiverr are great to start and build your portfolio. However, you'll be competing until

you're charging pennies for your highly-skilled work.

Instead of applying and taking any freelance work, find a specialization in your skill and keep on improving it.

For example, there are many specializations in writing and it's hard to stick out. Pick a specialization such as social media and email campaigns to hone. A specific niche is where you can find the most money. When you build up your skills to a high level in that specialization, you can charge a real rate and look for clients that want your "product". Remember to pick your specialization wisely and one that people want.

- *Attract Your Clients*
  You need to attract clients that will value your work and give you referrals to future clients. When you're starting off, try a few different types of projects to "test" if that's the specialization you want. Also, this is a chance to "test" if these are the types of clients you want to work with. Clients of similar projects work the same way and are connected.

  It's hard to turn down clients since you want to make money. However, working with clients in your niche is better in the long-run. Your work will be high-quality, which may result in repeat or referral clients.

- *Set Strategic Prices*
  Keep in mind, you need to set your prices based on your work's value, not your competitor's prices.

When you target the right clients, they will want to pay your price. And, you want to work for them because they value you and will pay you well. If it's a good business, they will make it work.

- *Build a Portfolio Website*
  You need a place to "show off" your work to potential clients. There, they can see the best of your work and any recommendations or comments previous clients have for you.
  In addition, you need to convey your services and who benefits from them.
  After the business part of your portfolio website, you need to market yourself.

- *Create Examples for Your Portfolio Website*
  Regularly update your portfolio website with new work from clients.
  If you don't have any new clients, create samples of services you offer. You can pretend it was from a client. Remember, these samples need to be what a potential client would want to pay for so pick wisely.

- *Choose Your Clients Sensibly*
  When you're first freelancing, you might not have enough time to "hunt" down clients and deliver high-quality work.
  Take the time to carefully pick clients in your specialization that will help you advance as a freelancer.

- *Give a Shout Out to Potential Clients in Your Work*

It's hard to get your name out there when you first start freelancing.

If you can, mention potential clients you'd like to work for such as companies, brands, or people.

It doesn't matter if you're ready to work with them or not. It will help down the line. Whenever you mention a potential client in your work, reach out to them and let them know. In your email, have a call to action such as "could you take a look at my work?". You'll most likely get a generic email back; however, you've now established a connection.

- *The Online "Elevator Script"*

  Have you heard about the one-minute elevator script?

  It's commonly used at job fairs to "sell" yourself to potential employers.

  For freelancers, you need this when you submit a proposal or an initial email to clients.

  In the proposal, you need to highlight your strengths, skills, and values when you first reach out. In addition, you must anticipate any questions they may have, provide samples, and have a nice layout in your proposal or initial email.

- *Keep Your Day Job*

  Don't prioritize freelancing over your day job. Remember, you still need to provide some type of living for yourself and while you freelance.

Remember, to be a successful freelancer, it takes time, patience, and a lot of work! I still have my day jobs and nowhere close to quitting. I don't always have time to take on a lot of clients. Instead, I go after a couple who can give me work I enjoy doing.

Chapter 7: Returning Home

At some point on your travels, you'll realize you want to go back home. Even if you settled down somewhere, you'll want to go home.

There are many reasons why you decide to end your travels, either temporarily or permanently. It could be that you're tired of traveling from place to place. Or, your money is running low. Or, you just want to be home.

There's never a right or wrong answer. You have to listen to yourself and figure out if the time is right or not.

This part of the book will help you adjust back to life after traveling.

It's harder in ways you expect and don't expect.

Use this part to help guide you. If you need more help, look to online forums or even a therapist.

What to Expect

Coming home from traveling is hard. There's no other way to put it.

You'll go from being frustrated to angry to feeling content with staying in one spot.

"Frozen in Time"

You think that while you're gone your hometown, friends, and family will have changed.

But, they won't.

Your friends will be working in the same field, going to the same bars and hangout spots. They will still be the same people when you left them before your travels.

Your hometown will still have the same feeling and vibe as a before. There will still be your favorite local restaurants, serving the same food and atmosphere. A few new buildings might be there when you return.

The only person that will have changed is *you*.

You'll still love your hometown, friends, family, but you'll feel foreign in your own home.

You want to continue to live as a traveler: try new things, meet new people, go to new places even in your hometown.

But no one seems to share that fiery passion as much as you. Only other travelers will. When you try to talk to your friends about this frustration, they can't help or relate to you. Your parents might be able to help if they were once travelers.

All you want to do is get back out on the road. Others will ask "Don't you like your hometown?" or "How can you think of leaving again when you just got back?".

Don't ever let someone convince you that saving up to travel again is wrong. Stay strong and find that inner fire that made you travel in the first place.

Before you know it, you'll be traveling again. Who knows, maybe this time, you'll be able to find a place to settle and work.

__Reverse Culture Shock__

Ever heard of reverse culture shock?

It's not as well-known or talked about as culture shock.

Some travelers don't ever experience any type of culture shock until they come home.

Reverse culture shock is common among post-travelers.

Here's the general idea of reverse culture shock:

When you become used to a new culture, it becomes a part of your identity. Small changes that you have incorporated into your life now are a part of your identity. Without even realizing it, these subtle new changes are now your familiar.

After living abroad, your hometown will seem different from your expat life. Your hometown might be different from when you left and may not be what you expect.

A few hurdles you might face with reverse culture shock:

- People aren't interested in hearing about your travels as much as you want to tell them about it.
- You aren't interested in hearing about things back home as your friends want to tell you about it.
- You miss being not home.
- You miss being among travelers.

How to Adjust

Adjusting to post-travel life is also hard in addition to dealing with reverse culture shock and anything else that makes you feel unsettled.

What can you do to help ease this while you save up for your next travels?

First, take a deep breath. Take your time adjusting to places and people who used to be familiar.

Find a cheap place to live, either friends or family's place.

Look for and get any job to pay the bills. It will let you feel at least financially stable. You can look for a better one down the line.

Seek out things to do outside of work that will keep you happy. They can be social, nonsocial activities, or both!

Start brainstorming activities you like doing, hobbies you want to learn or work on a personal project. This will help meet new people and is good for your mental health. You want to travel again, but don't burn yourself out by working so many hours a week.

Also, keep in touch with your traveling friends. You can reach out to them if they've returned home. They will know exactly what you're going through and give you some advice.

Saving Up Again

When you return home or even as you're traveling home, you'll probably think about leaving again and how to save enough to go.

This is normal and is encouraged!

Remember, those tips I wrote concerning how to save money?

It's in the first chapter.

If you don't feel like flipping to the beginning of the guide, here are a few I mentioned previously:

- **Learn to cook and make coffee for yourself**: Both will lower your monthly food bill!

- **Roommates:** If you still enjoy living with others, find a roommate or move into a place that needs one. It will cut down on your living expenses. If you want and still have the option, you can move back in with your parents.

- **Downgrade your phone plan:** Look for cheaper carriers that have the same coverage as the popular ones. Some may even let you own your phone instead of renting one.

- **Second-hand Store:** If you must buy new clothes, look for them at second-hand stores. They're far cheaper and you may find unique items there.

- **Sell Your Things:** If you have a pile of unwanted clothes or furniture, if you're living on your own, just sell it. You won't need it and putting it into a storage locker is another expense.

- **Cut Back on Drinking:** I know you may like having a drink with your friends at the end of the week, but alcohol is expensive. Drink either before you go out or just don't drink at all.

- **Don't Buy Pads and Tampons:** Pads and tampons cost at least $40/month for your period. Instead, buy a menstrual cup. Not only does it save you money it also helps the environment. Keep in mind, if you decide to visit remote places, you won't be able to walk up to the corner store. If you are able and want to, go on birth control that prevents you from having a period.

Staying in Touch with Friends You Meet

Staying in touch with the friends you made is great! Not only does it help ease reverse culture shock, it's nice to hear from someone you met months ago.

Of course, you don't have to stay in touch with everyone, just a few you felt especially close to. And, it doesn't have to be frequent either. A nice "How are you?" every few months is perfect.

You never know, a friend might be coming through your country and wants to visit or vice versa.

It's also incredibly comforting to have a piece of your travels while you're home. It gives you a glimmer of what you once had and will have.

Conclusion

When, or if, you return from your travels, you'll look back and say "wow, I did that, I learned this, and here's what I'm going to do next."

Traveling does amazing things for you and I can't wait for you to discover them!

About the Expert

Rebecca Friedberg graduated from The Ohio State University in 2017 where she pursued a degree in Classical Languages and a minor in Business Administration. After graduating, she traveled the world solo for six months.

Her travels took her to Spain, France, Germany, and Romania in Europe. In Asia, she traveled to Nepal, Thailand, Cambodia, and Vietnam.

Rebecca decided to travel after her first year in university. She knew that traveling held endless and valuable life-lessons she couldn't learn at school.

While in school, she saved her money, committed to the idea of traveling the world, and then made it a reality for herself.

She wrote this guide to pass along advice she was given and help future female solo world travelers.

This is Rebecca's second guide with HowExperts. For her first one, her topic was how to trek through the Manaslu Mountains of Nepal. In the future, Rebecca hopes to write other works and travel.

HowExpert publishes quick 'how to' guides on all topics from A to Z by everyday experts. Visit HowExpert.com to learn more.

Recommended Resources

- HowExpert.com – Quick 'How To' Guides on All Topics from A to Z by Everyday Experts.
- HowExpert.com/free – Free HowExpert Email Newsletter.
- HowExpert.com/books – HowExpert Books
- HowExpert.com/courses – HowExpert Courses
- HowExpert.com/membership – HowExpert Membership Site
- HowExpert.com/writers – Write About Your #1 Passion/Knowledge/Expertise & Become a HowExpert Author.
- HowExpert.com/resources – Additional HowExpert Recommended Resources
- YouTube.com/HowExpert – Subscribe to HowExpert YouTube.
- Instagram.com/HowExpert – Follow HowExpert on Instagram.
- Facebook.com/HowExpert – Follow HowExpert on Facebook.

Printed in Great Britain
by Amazon